T0147472

Towards A
Scientific Theory of Culture

Towards A
Scientific Theory of Culture

The writings of Bronislaw Malinowski

By Oscar Fernández

ISBN: 978-1-4669-1180-2 (sc)
ISBN: 978-1-4669-1181-9 (e)

Trafford rev. 01/19/2012

 www.trafford.com

North America & international
toll-free:1 888 232 4444 (USA & Canada)
phone:250 383 6864 ♦ fax:812 355 4082

ACKNOWLEDGMENTS

I am grateful to a series of Social Anthropology professors and lecturers for their observations on this study, which have without doubt contributed to improving the manuscript. Formerly, and in order to finish the text, I visited the *London School of Economics and Political Science*, at the University of London, in order to consult the *Malinowski Archive*. Here I would like to express my debt of gratitude to Professor Charles Stafford, Coordinator of the LSE Department of Anthropology, at whose invitation I was able to visit the Department. I would also like to thank Dr. Michael Young, the official biographer of Malinowski and professor at the National University of Australia, for his comments, above all with regard to some of the figures included in the book. Lastly, it would be an injustice not to mention here the Archive staff at the *British Library of Political and Economic Science (LSE)*, for their patience and dedication, and especially Mrs. Sue Donnelly. Mr. Philip Cook. merits a separate mention. To all of you, many thanks.

CONTENTS

1. INTRODUCTION

Bronislaw Malinowski was a man of enigmas and contradictions, and the author of what is probably the most famous, mythologised and extensive field work ever conducted in the history of anthropology. He was the man who undertook a paradigmatic journey to a paradigmatic destination, the anthropologist who discovered a method just as he was losing the object, the author who employed a new narrative style in his monographs describing his work on the natives of the Trobriand Islands, the scientist who, with his methodological innovations, became one of the proponents of the 19th century transformation of speculative anthropology into the modern Science of Humanity and the master who trained an entire generation of anthropologists whose studies and theories dominated the academic world. A consummate critic and polemicist, he attracted a wide and varied audience to anthropology. In sum, a man who, from the very beginnings of his intellectual labours, had a different perception of anthropology, as a science directed by direct research in the field, where theory and the search for general laws should be based on empirical research implying systematic observation and meticulous analysis of the actual behaviour of individuals in living, functioning societies.

In the course of this intellectual labour, he introduced a *functionalist focus* into the study of culture. He proposed that culture represented an integrated system of institutions which derived from human needs. The anthropologists' aim, he postulated, was to construct a 'Science of Culture'.

The key concept throughout his work was that of *function*, which, although basic, was always employed in a flexible and exploratory fashion, subject to revision, from his first studies published in *The Family among the Australian Aborigines* (1913) through to his posthumous work *The scientific theory of culture* (1944) where he produced a theoretical formulation of the concept. Above all he was interested in the study of culture as a universal phenomenon and the development of a theoretical framework which would enable him to undertake a systematic study of each culture in all its aspects and to conduct intercultural comparisons.

Despite the numerous studies which have been carried out on Malinowski's work, a full biography is still not available today, 60 years after his death. As R. Thornton and P. Skalník observed (1993:9), one reason for this may be that his roots, in which certain fundamental questions regarding his work are located, are still unknown. His complete bibliography contains over one hundred titles, and critical studies of his work are even more numerous. His work continues to command increasing interest, and an example of this would be the recently published book by M. Young (1998). New facts and texts are emerging which; fortunately, break with the stereotypes that for one reason or another have been attributed to Malinowski for some time.

In the present study, I will begin by remarking on some aspects of Malinowski's personal and professional trajectory. Next, I will discuss his early works, some of which were written in Polish and others in German and perhaps for this reason are less well known than the rest of his work, but which have recently been translated into English. In these, we will find some of the keys to later developments in his work. Following on, in the central section, I will review and assess those subjects to which he dedicated most of his efforts, such as the study of economics, kinship, magic and language, and will conclude with a discussion his last works, some of them published posthumously. It is not my intention here to produce a study of the complete works of Malinowski—a task as ambitious as it would be impossible—but rather, to explore some of the anthropologist's most interesting, and at times controversial, contributions. Indeed, some of the debates which arose as a result of his thought are still highly topical today.

1.1. Malinowski's personal and professional trajectory

Bronislaw Kasper Malinowski was born in Kraków, Poland, on the 7th of April, 1884, the only son of Lucjan Feliks Jan Malinowski and Josefa Née Lacka. The Malinowski family belonged to the Polish nobility, but had long since ceased to possess any outward sign that would indicate this. As Kuper commented (1978:5), Malinowski would recall these noble origins with a mixture of humour, irony and vanity.

His father was an eminent philologist and folklorist who was determined to establish a School for Slovakian Folklore Studies in Kraków. At that time, Kraków formed part, politically speaking, of the Austro-Hungarian Empire. Given that the intellectual and cultural life of the times was marked by the influence of Russia and Germany, Lucjan Malinowski elected the latter and obtained his doctorate in Leipzig in 1872. He began teaching at the Kraków Academy in 1867, but in 1877 moved to the Jagiellonian University in Kraków, founded in 1364 and one of the oldest universities in Eastern Europe, where he began to teach comparative linguistics of the Slav languages, focusing on the dialects and ethnography of Silesia. Lucjan Malinowski died in 1898, when his son was fourteen years old (Borowska, 1971:3-4).

Bronislaw Malinowski was always frail, suffering from poor eyesight and respiratory problems. In 1901, when he was 17 years old, he underwent an operation on his eyes which obliged him to suspend his studies for a while. From that point onwards, his mother would play an important role in his studies and education (Flis, 1985:249). He was dogged by illness throughout his life, to the extent that he was compelled to change his professional direction and seek in anthropology a new object of intellectual interest. Illness also obliged him to undertake a series of journeys to warmer climes, accompanied by his mother, and these took him to North Africa, Italy, Madeira and the Canary Isles where, years later, he would return to write his monograph *Argonauts of the Western Pacific.*,

In 1902 he was admitted to the Jagellonian University, with all the honours which accrued from being the son of one of the University's own professors. There he studied philosophy, and four years later, defended his thesis.

As G. Kubica (1988:102-103) remarked, to judge by his academic curriculum, or *Index Lectionnum*, his initial studies focused on physics and mathematics, and later on philosophy and psychology. His mathematics courses included analytical geometry, calculus and logic whilst those in physics dealt with electricity, magnetism and heat. The study of teaching, psychology, ethics, social politics, Slav ethnology and philosophy allowed him to explore the sociological literature on the family, religion, work and kinship.

From 1906 onwards, he combined his studies with a series of journeys. He travelled to Italy, and then returned to sit his final examinations in philosophy and physics (Flis, 1985:248). And in July of the same year, he completed his doctoral thesis entitled "On the principle of the economy of thought". Once again, without waiting for graduation, he embarked on another journey, this time to the Canary Isles, in the hope that his health would improve.

In 1908, he received his doctorate *sub auspiciis imperatoris* (Kubica, 1988:95), and went on to study at Leipzig, where he worked with Wilhelm Wundt, the father of experimental psychology and a recognised master in the field of anthropology due to his work on the 'psychology of the people' (Völker-psychologie), and his work with the famous historian and economist of the times, Karl Bücher. The latter's deep interest in primitive economies inspired a similar interest in Malinowski, which would culminate in his first monograph, *Argonauts of the Western Pacific*.

Later, he declared his intention of going to England for at least a year in order to 'improve his qualifications', and arrived in 1910. He studied in London for almost four years. It was during this period that he wrote some book reviews in Polish, including one on Frazer's *Totemism and Exogamy*, and his book *Primitive Religion and Forms of Social Structure*, published in 1915.

In London, he studied at the London School of Economics (LSE) under E. Westermarck, A. C. Haddon, W. H. R. Rivers and C. G. Seligman. Thanks to the help of the latter, he received the Robert Mond travelling scholarship from the University of London and the Constance Hutchinson scholarship from the LSE, which enabled him to travel to New Guinea.

It was also in London where he published his first book in English, *The Family among the Australian Aborigines* published in 1913 and based on bibliographical research, a clear example of Malinowski's sociological method. In the book, he examined the role that the social institution of the family played in the maintenance of social order. He did not employ the evolutionary approach of historical reconstruction, but neither did he explicitly reject such an approach.

This 'preparatory' period concluded with his article *A Fundamental Problem of Religious Society*, which he presented in New Guinea in 1914, to the British Society for Advanced Studies at its Australian headquarters.

In September of 1914 he set out on his first expedition, with the aim of studying the Mailu people of Toulon Island, and stayed there until February 1915. His ethnographic report of this field work, *The Natives of Mailu* (1915), won him a doctorate in science from the LSE, awarded in 1916. Shortly after, he was to condemn this study. The Mailu seemed "vulgar and not very intelligent" to him (Malinowski, 1922:34), and his interest was instead captured by what he had heard of the Massim people, who lived further to the east.

From June 1915 to May 1016 he embarked on his second expedition which took him, almost by chance, to the Trobriand Islands. He had not been there long before he was able to dispense with the services of an interpreter and speak the native language, Kiriwina, himself. However, it was not until his second visit, from October 1917 to October 1918, by which time he had systemised his notes from his first year there, that he was able to follow a rapid conversation and take notes in this language (Metraux, 1979:732).

Between one journay and the other, he wrote his first description of the culture, *Baloma:the Spirit of the Dead in the Trobriand Islands,* published in 1916. With hindsight, it is possible to see that in this work he had found his subject, his working style and his characteristic mode of expression.

The death of his mother in 1920, during his second visit to the Trobriand Islands, had a very profound effect on him, and at some point during this career he would acknowledge the important role that she had played in his education and training.

On his return to Europe in 1920, he married Elsie Masson, a British woman who had been born and raised in Australia and with whom he had three daughters, Josefa, Wanda and Helena. This woman, too, was to be of no small importance to his professional career, helping him in his work and reading and discussing his writings.

Thus, from the combination of his knowledge, his education, principally in European philosophy, and his innovative, lengthy field work in New Guinea, Malinowski created a new approach to anthropology which would quickly be taken up by his students throughout the Commonwealth. Malinowski's career as one of the founders of British social anthropology had just begun.

In 1920, he began to teach at the LSE. In 1924, he was named professor, and three years later he was asked to become the first Professor of Anthropology at the University of London.

His position as a scientist of international renown was launched with the publication in 1922 of *Argonauts of the Western Pacific*. The following 15 years, from 1923 to 1938, were his most productive as a researcher, writer, theoretician and, above all, as a brilliant and controversial teacher, who played a leading role in the creation of the British School of Social Anthropology.

He stimulated and taught an entire generation of young anthropologists, including E. E. Evans-Pritchard, Raymond Firth, Meyer Fortes, Hogbin, Phyllis Kaberry,

Hortense Powdermaker, Edmund Leach, Lucy Mair, Ashley Montagu, S. F. Nadel, Talcott Parsons, Audrey Richards, Isaac Schapera, Godfrey Wilson and many more, all of whom quickly enriched both the anthropological world and the ethnographic literature, establishing what Murdock (1943:442) called "a new level of excellence". In 1934, he spent three months in Africa visiting his students in the field. Some of these described him as a brilliant speaker whilst others thought he was a boring teacher and still others became his fiercest critics and detractors. His classes were both a place for debate and discussion of his works, and a training ground for colonial agents of the British government. Audrey I. Richards (1943:3) described the relationship between Malinowski and his students as follows: "he tended to think of them, more than as a series of individuals with different interests and needs, as a team fighting on the same side. They learnt a particular working method and a particular theoretical approach rather than a collection of detailed facts. (. . .) It was in the seminars where he best displayed his talent for teaching. These weekly discussions became famous and attracted many different types of students. Colonial administrators on leave were interested by Malinowski's lively and direct approach. (. . .) Researchers from all over the world attended and he often reeled off sentances in four or five languages. Side by side with university lecturers sat simple enthusiasts, and he had the rare quality of being able to awaken ideas in others. (. . .) His students could become irritated with his intolerance or inspired by his enthusiasm."

In 1938, he went to the United States of America on a year's sabbatical. This was not his first visit, and previous occasions had included a period at the University of California in 1926 on the invitation of Laura Spelman Rockefeller Memorial Insitution, where he visited the Hopi

Indians of the southeast, Cornell University in 1933, and in 1936, acting as the representative of the University of London, he attended the commemoration of Harvard University's third centenary and was awarded the title of *Doctor honoris causa*.

It was during this new trip, where he was to teach at Yale University and later at the Bishop Museum, that the Second World War broke out and he was obliged to remain. As Rhoda Métraux (1979:734) observed, his position in the United States was not easy: "He was a foreigner, his work was not so well known, his students were less prepared than his students in London and the need to start teaching from scratch depressed him". This lack of interest can be seen in the simplified version that he gave of his theoretical system in *A Scientific Theory of Culture*, his most famous posthumous work, published in 1944.

In 1940, the year in which he entered into his second marriage, to the painter Valletta Swann, he began a new project in collaboration with Julio de la Fuente. This consisted in the study of market trade between the Zapoteca people of Oaxaca. Despite his failing health, he travelled to Oaxaca in the summers of 1940 and 1941. The following year, in 1942, he was named permanent professor at Yale. He died on the 16ᵗʰ of May of the same year.

1.2. The intellectual climate of the times.

The intellectual climate in which Malinowski began to develop his interest in anthropology was marked by two paradigms which were just entering into decline:evolutionism and a mechanistic version of materialism (Panoff,1974:7). Partially due to the influence of authors such as Lewis Morgan with his work *Ancient Society*, which impregnated the works of James Frazer, Franz Boas or Edward

Westermarck, the hypothesis that all humanity had followed a single evolutionary line formed the basis of anthropological orthodoxy in England.

This sociological evolutionism was no more than a transposition of biological evolutionism. However, such an approach required these authors to juggle with the order of events, something which was not to their liking and they consequently tended towards *diffusionism*. The case of Rivers is, perhaps, the most evident. What these authors offered was a 'speculative history', an intellectual endeavour against which Malinowski directed severe criticism throughout his works. In order to appreciate the extent to which this trend was influential, we can cite the fact that even Freud, despite his independent spirit, adopted social evolutionary theory in *Totem and Taboo* (1913), a book to which Malinowski gave considerable attention.

The second intellectual trend of the times which also aroused the hostility of Malinowski was mechanistic materialism, of which Wundt, Malinowski's mentor at Leipzig, was a source. From the beginnings of the 19th century, this theory underlay the different association theories in psychology.

When Malinowski arrived in England, other ideas had come to the fore, especially the psychology of William James. E. R. Leach (1974:293) indicated that it was in the work of William James that Malinowski found the inspiration which would prove to be the most fertile as regards his later intellectual development, since earlier influences, precisely for their negative effect, rendered the need for a synthesis even more imperative. Indeed, the increasing closeness between the ethnographer and the psychologist became all the more convincing when considering the notion of pragmatism and the role this played in the work of both. Like William James, in his theoretical writings Malinowski not only turned to pragmatism to provide an ultimate explanation of human behaviour, but also formulated it in similar terms.

With the publication of *Principles* in 1890, William James developed the idea of functionalism in psychology, and curiously, would receive the same criticisms from his successors as Malinowski. Such criticism was particularly directed at the very concept of function which, due to its inherent ambiguity, fluctuated between a biological definition (or tautological, for the severest critics) and a teleological one, or the idea of a final purpose (that is to say, not scientific).

Later, behavioural psychology would exercise its influence on Malinowski, but until 1935, with the publication of *Coral Gardens*, he did not openly declare his support.

Other theoreticians of the time, such as Durkheim, who had a lasting influence on Great Britain, did not particularly arouse Malinowski's interest. It would appear that he gave Durkheim's work a superficial reading, according to Firth (1981:134), or at least without feeling any intellectual affinity with what he read, despite the fact that in later years he would cite Durkheim profusely and even designated him as one of the founding fathers of anthropology, to the extent of naming him as a precursor of functionalism (Malinowski, 1944:148). More surprising was his apparent ignorance of Max Weber, although on this point it should be remembered that both Durkheim and Mauss also appeared to be unaware of him despite their more open outlook.

Evolutionism, diffusionism, the psychology of William James, Durkheimian sociology and psychoanalysis were the principal influences on Malinowski whilst he sought his own direction.

Turning from the intellectual climate of the times to the state of anthropology in that period, four developments clearly indicate how far the discipline had advanced before Malinowski's arrival in London (Panoff, 1974:21).

Firstly, the growing interest among philosophers, sociologists and historians in the information compiled on primitive peoples. Secondly, aware of this new intellectual concern, universities gave official status to the study of primitive peoples, under the name of ethnology or anthropology, achieving official recognition as a discipline at Oxford in 1884, Cambridge in 1900, and London in 1908. Thirdly, it had become an accepted principle that it was no longer possible to rely on the occasional curiosity of travellers or missionaries to collect ethnographic data, but that anthropologists should collect their information themselves from *in situ* observation, necessarily implying 'field work'. Such a need had already been pointed out in the mid 19th century by Lewis H. Morgan, in his work on the Iroquois, and thirty years later by Fran Boas, reporting on various periods spent among the Eskimos and the Kwakwaka'wakw (formerly known as the Kwakiutl). Lastly, it should be noted that this example did not gain wide-spread acceptance until the initiative of Haddon, organiser of the 1898-99 expedition to the Torres Strait. Despite its deficiencies, this journey marked a turning point in the history of anthropology due to the number and status of its members and the impetus it gave to empirical research. Participants included Rivers, Radcliffe-Brown and Seligman, a fact which indicates the extent of the growing interest mentioned above.

Thus, when Malinowski travelled to the Trobriand Islands in 1914, this tradition was already firmly rooted in the discipline and his journey did not constitute a novelty. However, what his work did represent was a contribution to the theory and practice of field work. Nevertheless, it was thanks to the influence of Durkheim that British anthropology began to take a sociological approach, shaking off its former dependence on 'material culture and intrepid behaviour' in the style of Frazer.

1.3. Bronislaw Malinowski's early works

Malinowski's early works represent an intense theoretical endeavour prior to his departure from Europe to commence field work in the Trobriand Islands. They constitute some pieces of the jigsaw of Europe's confrontation with the 'savage', of the 'Self' with 'the Other', and of the adaptation of European social sciences and philosophy, among many other issues which went beyond field work itself.

In order to comment on these texts, I have used the compilation entitled *The early writings of Broniwslaw Malinowski Malinowski's writings, 1904-1914*, edited by Robert J. Thornton and Peter Skalník (1993) using translations into English by Ludwik Krzyzanowski, since the texts were originally written in Polish, Malinowski's mother tongue, and to a lesser extent, German. Despite indications in his correspondence of Malinowski's desire to see these texts translated into English, especially during the period immediately following his arrival at the London School of Economics, for various reasons this was never carried out. The texts include 'Observations on Friedrich Nietzsche's *The Birth of Tragedy*' from 1904-5, his doctoral thesis 'On the principle of economy of thought' from 1906, 'Religion and magic:*The Golden Bough*' (1910) and 'Totemism and exogamy' (1911-1913), two texts criticising the thought of Frazer, 'Tribal male associations in Australia' (1912), 'The economic aspects of the *intichiuma* ceremonies' (1912), 'The relationship of primitive beliefs to the forms of social organisation' (1913), 'A fundamental problem of religious sociology' (1914), and 'Sociology of the family' (1913-1914), a series of texts based on information about the Australian Aborigines.

These texts indicate the route by which Malinowski arrived at the theories which defined the data he collected, data which, in turn, have defined a large part of the subject matter of anthropology ever since. Furthermore, all display a clear and consistent relationship, and through them can be witnessed the trajectory of Malinowski's thought, from the philosophy of Nietzsche to the critical empiricism of Mach and what he himself defined as the 'provocative errors of Frazer', culminating in Malinowski's modern anthropology project.

I would like to emphasise that this investigation into what could be called the 'Polish roots' of ethnography does not imply that all possible questions were addressed from the beginning, but rather that these roots form the genealogy of some of the problems which continue to influence the characteristics of modern anthropologists' ethnographies.

The influence of Nietzsche on the work of Malinowski was unknown until Skalník discovered a manuscript written in 1904 among Malinowski's paper held at the University of Yale. This is a dense and passionate essay on Nietzche's *Birth of Tragedy*, which introduced a new dimension into Malinowski's thought. R. Thornton and P. Skalník (1993:4) considered the influence of Nietzche to be the 'missing link' between the positivism or philosophical pragmatism of Mach and *Myth in Primitive Psychology* (1925), *Crime and Custom in Savage Society* (1926), *Coral Graden and their Magic* (1935) and *Freedom and Civilisation* (1947). Apart from a few brief references in his field notes and other obscure publications (Malinowski 1937:133-168; 1962), Malinowski appears never to have mentioned Nietzsche.

These writings show that Malinowski's ideas emerged from a rich European tradition which he then adapted and partially transformed. Perhaps because he wished to proclaim himself prophet of the new anthropology, he never mentioned these influences in his writings in English. In contrast, whilst he did acknowledge the influence of Frazer, Seligman and Westermarck, the nature and direction of this influence is not clear from the few brief footnotes which he included. Furthermore, whereas in his English writings he paid homage to the influence of Frazer (Malinowski, 1925; 1944), in his Polish works he made it very clear that Frazer's importance stemmed chiefly from the "transparency of his errors" and from being an "indigestible archive of ethnographic information", with methodological embellishments. Thus, to a certain extent, Frazer taught Malinowski how 'not to be an anthropologist'. But this is only clear from his writings in Polish, written long before he realised that he would need Frazer's support in England.

Malinowski's first essays, then, show the influence of three great thinkers, Nietzsche, Mach and Frazer, as summarised in Table 1. Malinowski's comments regarding Nietzsche's essay on *The Birth of Tragedy* suggest that it was Nietzsche more than Frazer who influenced his crucial decision to direct his career towards the science of society. Nietzsche provoked in Malinwski the question of how to conduct science, in which Mach, the question of knowledge and error, and the technical and procedural problems of science all figured. Together, these perspectives clarified for Malinowski the basic problems and conventionalisms of European science, to the extent that when he met Frazer, he was already intellectually prepared to overcome the limitations that Frazer himself placed on his own theoriesEthnography's simplistic notion of a direct evolution from magic to religion and science, with its lack of rigour, naïve faith in the ethnographic reports produced by all kinds of amateurs and tolerance for the multiple and contradictory conclusions of its own productions, was attacked and rejected in all its aspects by Malinowski. Nevertheless, the fundamental questions raised by Frazer remained latent, questions to which Nietzsche and Mach had little to contribute. Thus, according to R. Thornton and P. Skalník (1993), "it would not be an exaggeration to say that Malinowski's ethnography developed through the application of a synthesis of Nietzsche and Mach's thought with Frazer's ethnographic project". The problems erroneously raised by Frazer are not resolved but rather, reformulated in the light of contemporary thought, making them appear valid. Malinowski went beyond the limits of Frazer's discourse in order to raise questions such as "Does totemism really exist?", "Doesn't magic actually form a practice or techniques rather than an intellectual category?", "Can we uncover the origins of a belief or part of a culture?", and finally, "¿What do we mean by 'belief', by 'part of a culture', or even by 'origins', precisely?". The concrete result of all these questions was a series of detailed ethnographic studies, methodological treatises and philosophical formulations which both rejected an ethnographic discourse and founded another anthropological discourse dealing with questions such as the concepts of 'myth as charter', the function of culture as a whole, reciprocity in social relationships, the nature of values, the fiction of kinship, linguistic pragmatism and many other vigorous ideas and important problems.

From the beginning, Malinowski applied aspects of Nietzsche's approach and in particular, the methods described in *The Birth of Tragedy* and *On the Genealogy of Morals*; the themes of myth, morality, sexuality, punishment, the nature of power and order in the midst of apparent chaos, the nature and power of knowledge and the relationship between words and things, formed a tangible presence throughout his work, from his first to his last publications. As Gellner observed (1988), Malinowski's concerted effort suggests a deliberate attempt to impose his own stamp on anthropology, whilst declaring that "his old gods were, if not dead, at least in decline, suggests a Zarathustra in the London School of Economics, more than an Argonaut or even a Zeno of Kraków".

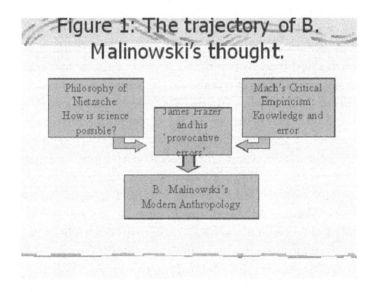

Figure 1: The trajectory of B. Malinowski's thought.

Observations on *The Birth of Tragedy* by Nietzsche (1904-5)

The *Birth of Tragedy* was Nietzsche's first published work, and it both reflects the enthusiasm of the young writer and reveals the topics which would later obssess the philosopher and would reappear, above all, in *On the Genealogy of Morals*. Likewise, Malinowski's essay on this work by Nietzsche formed one of his earliest writings as a student. Even so, it introduces ideas which would provide the direction for his research throughout the rest of his life.

The essay was written in the period 1904-05, probably for a course on "The Philosophy of Nietzsche". Although Malinowski never published or referred to it, he always kept it among his papers and took it with him on his last trip to America, where it was later found by Peter Skalník in 1980 (the published version of the text referred to here is from R. Thornton and P. Skalník, 1993).

According to R. Thornton and P. Skalník (1993), the essay provides various crucial keys to understanding the sources and motives behind Malinowski's theoretical and ethnographic work. It reveals that the roots of the influence behind Malinowski's 'myth as charter' theory and his supposed ahistoricism lie in his attempt to understand Nietzsche's revolutionary approach to classical tragedy and mythology. These ideas reemerged throughout his ethnographic writings, essays and even in his personal correspondence. This essay on Nietzsche enables us to locate Malinowski's work much more firmly within the iintellectual and philosophical tradition to which it belongs, and therefore, to gain a better understanding of the nature of his approaches. This insight into his intellectual development also represents a significant contribution to the development of functionalism and the importance of social anthropology in the social and human sciences in the 20th century.

It would seem that Malinowski conducted a critical reading of Nietzsche. He carefully rejected many of his considerations and perspectives, but took from him a new and fertile concept of myth and a particular approach to history. Nietzsche's essay is both a type of myth about texts and a text about myth. According to R. Thornton and P. Skalník (1993:16) in their attempt to clarify our understanding of Malinowski, what is surprising, given that these ideas reappear in his field work, "is the direct social confrontation between Malinowski and the natives of Australia, Mailu and Kiriwina, with Nietzsche lodged in some part of his mind".

As regards structure, the essay is divided into five parts. In the first, he defined 'metaphysics' and presented his criticism of Schopenhauer's, and thus of Nietzsche's, approach to metaphysics. In the second part, he introduced his own concept of myth and presented *The Birth of Tragedy* as a myth about myth. "This book", said Malinowski, "is in itself, as a form of creativity, a concept of thought, a myth". The third part is of particular interest today, as Malinowski gave a 'functional' reading of Nietzsche's main critical categories and developed some ideas conerning the inter-relationships between art, myth and metaphysics. In the fourth section, he looked at Nietzsche's ability as an artist, but indicated that the part of Nietzsche's work which would endure was not his artistic ability but rather his examination of the question of the nature of tragedy in relation to thought, life and art. In the fifth part, Malinowski presented his most important question, which refers to the psychological function of art and the relationship of thought (as science) with tragedy (as myth). Lastly, in the conclusion, Malinowski indicated some of the keys to his reading of Nietzsche for future research.

As regards the first topic addressed, metaphysics, Malinowski began with a critique of Nietzsche's dependence on the metaphysics of Schopenhauer. He pointed out that Nietzsche's construction stood or fell according to the validity of Schopenhauer's metaphysics. Malinowski understood metaphysics as an attempt to anthropomorphise the world of objective reality, and argued that German metaphysics in general, and that of Nietzsche, of *The Birth of Tragedy*, in particular, represented an attempt to subjectivise or humanise the objective world of things. Thus, whilst "from a purely scientific point of view, metaphysics possesses a system of exact and pure concepts (. . .), the philosophical ends of (the questions of) metaphysics cannot be attained or addressed", since the simple anthropomorphisation of the world cannot create "a world from human reality". The ultimate reality of the objective world would be 'forever closed' to the word of thought and emotions. However, Malinowski argued that metaphysics was a "universal symptom of the human soul", since humans need to understand their environment in human terms, which implies that it must be given human form. Therefore, concepts such as the Christian *God*, Hegel's *Geist*, Leibniz's *Monads* or Schopenhauer's *Will*, among others, all represented attempts to understand the world as if it were human. And since the world is not human, all failed to attain this true knowledge.

R. Thornton and P. Skalník (1993) stated that Malinowski's inspiration for his critique of Nietzsche came from two sources. First, the belief that 'objective reality' can never penetrate human consciousness but can only be described and conceptualised, which was one of the precepts or dogmas of Ernest Mach's empiricism. More problematically, however, was the assertion that metaphysics was simply the anthropomorphisation of the world. Similar arguments were used by Auguste Comte in his first formulations of the doctrine of positivism, and were later taken up by James Frazer, Wilhelm Wundt and Adolf Bastian. All these used this notion to characterise primitive religion, rather than European metaphysics. Malinowski was sufficiently audacious, or daring, however, to apply this to Nietzsche. In a later essay, he explicitly compared the Catholic mass to the rituals of primitive religion, and his (reflexive) use of ethnographic arguments in this manner clearly represented a critical and challenging stance on his part.

As regards the second topic, Malinowski argued that art, metaphysics and myth were 'genetically related'. By this, he meant that they arose from the same motivations rather than having the same origins. All were based on the existence of the unavoidable dichotomies which are characteristic of the structure of the human mind, and all enabled leaps to be made between different classes and orders of reality. In other words, they represented fundamental 'functions' of the human mind. This statement made it clear that Malinowski had extracted myth from the 'past' and had begun to consider it a functional element of the present. This, in and of itself, could be considered a notable achievement, namely, the idea that myth is a constitutive element of the present derived from the past. Malinowski first defined myth as a "category referring to the historic past", but opposed the idea of myth as "pure history", in terms of a reconstruction of events, on the one hand, and as "scientific history" (sociology) seeking "laws of historical evolution", on the other. According to Malinowski's way of thinking, myth on this level was characterised by the "personification of ideals", "images of the past (. . .) drawn from another dimension". On this point, R. Thornton and P. Skalník (1993:22) remarked that in contrast to Nietzsche, Malinowski universalised the concept of myth, turning it into a universal form of knowledge, not only one type of knowledge but rather something which was always different and always present. Conceived of as a form of knowledge (a form of comprehension), they argued that for Malinowski and those who came after, the myth became a central aspect of anthropological method. In accordance with this view, myth had a function, a role in social life. Myth provided the explanation for what is, in terms of what was, but more than this, it "transforms the directness of emotion" into another dimension where the immediacy of pain and suffering is minimalised and consequently, alleviated.

Malinowski used the example of the Christian myth of the agony of Christ, but said that the mythic process, although not the content, "would be similar everywhere". In fact, this is what he attempted to show in his essay on *Tribal male associations in Australia* (1912) and in his first text on the Trobriand Islands, *Baloma; the spirit of the dead in the Trobriand Islands* (1916).

Myth, he claimed, was a "concept of reality" and as such, engendered an intellectual method similar to metaphysics, genetically related to, although significantly different from, metaphysics. Whilst metaphysics referred to the relationship between thought and emotion, between appearance and reality, myth referred to the relationship between past and present. These words prefigured the definition of myth he gave, for example, in *Myth in Primitive Psychology* (1925), where he described myth as an affirmation of reality first, and of daily life, justified by what went before (and the past), which produced retrospecive patterns of moral values, sociological order and magical beliefs. Myth, he said, was no mere narrative, nor a form of science, nor a branch of art or history, nor an explanatory or educational tale. It fulfilled a *sui generis* function, closely related to the nature of tradition and the continuity of culture, with the relationship between generations (adults and children), and with human perspectives of the past (Malinowski, 1925:147).

One question which might come to mind is how it was possible that a young Pole and student of philosophy should be so critical of Nietzsche. How could he confront him and say "this means nothing to me"? Indeed, on this point R.

Thornton and P. Skalník (1993:25) argued that one of the most powerfully attractive aspects of Nietzsche was the sense of moral liberty he gave to his readers. Malinowski also acquired this sense of freedom from two other sources:from Ernst Mach and the school of critical empiricist thought which he studied at the Jagiellonian University in Kraków, and from the modernist movement known as Young Poland, with which he was associated. Thus, "functionalism was Malinowski's cure for the (nausea of) Nietzsche. His functionalism became, in fact, a method rather than a theory. The method consisted in using one's entire personal life as a scientific instrument which, as with any instrument, permitted the discovery of patterns and connections which were previously unseen. This method did not presuppose a transcendental idea, nor did it make the loss of all values disappear, even when old values were reassessed in the field, as long as there were lives to live, descriptions to write, and 'windows on the world from which we can look out and even, sometimes, see through" (*Ibid*).

On the Principle of the Economy of Thought (1906).

This was Malinowski's doctoral thesis. It is mainly of interest today because it demonstrates Malinowski's sharp philosophical insight together with the roots of his methodological innovations and his attitude towards science. The doctoral thesis of the young Malinowski represents, furthermore, a critical historical approach to two of the most representative figures of the anti-metaphysical movement in Europe:Richard Avenarius, the critical empiricist psychologist, and Ernst Mach, the methodologist. The main goal of his dissertation was to assess whether the principle of an economy of thought contained metaphysical assumptions or if it could be reduced to empirical elements.

The argument of the dissertation, which is relatively straightforward although the level of detail at times renders it complex and dense, refers to the possibilities and limitations of the notion of an 'economy of thought', as formulated by Richard Avenarius and Ernst Mach.

Ernst Mach was a physicist and historian who, although not overly concerned with developing an exhaustive history of ideas, was however interested in revising the descriptions which his discipline gave to the meanings and methods of history and criticism. Mach commenced his theory of science in a similar manner to Frazer, seeking comparable evidence in ethnology and history, in order to produce a more complete justification of science. Through his work on the history of thermodynamics and mechanics, Mach developed a widely influential philosophy of science, later called 'neo-positivism'. He believed that the world of the mind was essentially independent from the world of nature, and that science consisted in the construction of theories about nature. For Mach, theories were constructs or mental fictions:they remained part of the mind, not part of physical reality, and implied nothing about the true nature of the physical world, independent of the theories constructed around it. Science was exclusively based on the capacity of thought to organise and account for the experience of the senses, and this implied that we, literally, could not account for anything other than what could be directly experienced. Thus, Mach rejected the existence of atoms, arguing that the theories on which the concept of an atom was based only worked because they were economical representations of nature, not because atoms really existed. His conception of science was 'relativist' (R. Thornton and P. Skalník, 1993:28).

The 'economy of thought' refers to the elimination of any metaphysical concept from a description of the natural world. Metaphysical elements could be considered the most uneconomical for thought. Therefore, "Does metaphysics have a right to exist?" asked Malinowski at the beginning of his dissertation. This question could be considered one of the fundamental issues of his time, complex and at the same time creative. He was to conclude that it was empiricism that the social sciences needed, although on its own, this would be insufficient.

Another argument in the dissertation revolved around the concept of 'function', and in the first part, Malinowski attempted to use this concept in a strictly mathematical sense. The concept of function was also central to his evaluation of the principle of the economy of thought. As Flis (1988:124) observed, Malinowski used this concept to analyse the meaning of economy, which he defined as the *minimum* of function. Whilst the term as it is used in his dissertation did not carry the dynamic or psychological connotations that Malinowski would later give it, it helped to refine the concept of an abstract analytical space conceptualised as a set of relationships between the elements of sets, or as a set of relationships between parts. In other words, its sense was purely mathematical:the manner in which the elements of one set corresponded to another.

As mentioned earlier, Malinowski analysed the principle of the economy of thought as used by Richard Avenarius and Ernst Mach. In general, according to this principle, "the most correct thought is that which consumes less mental energy in understanding an infinitely complex world". Malinowski related the principle of the economy of thought to the principle of univocal determination. In nature, where it is assumed that the latter principle operates, it is not possible to speak of economy, and similarly, it would not be possible if there were only one way of adapting thought appropriately. The principle therefore rejects a deterministic and linear evolutionism. In completely determined and isolated systems, it is not possible to speak of economy, argued Malinowski. On the basis of this argument, he rejected the principle of Avenarius as metaphysical, since his conception of the human spirit was mechanical, namely, a completely determined and isolated entity and therefore in contradiction with the application of the principle of economy. On the contrary, Mach's principle was consistent given that, to the extent that it was methodological, it described the criteria necessary to assess scientific theories according to their efficiency by introducing the final purpose of the phenomena investigated. Thus, and in economic terms, the body's consumption of physiological energy and acquisition represents the adaptation of thought to the facts.

For Mach, valid knowledge was economic thought, that is, thought which did not assume the existence of unempirical, transcendental entities. This formed the basis of Malinowski's radical empiricism:an analysis of the world of culture cannot assume the existence of any unempirical transcendental entity. As G. W. Stocking (1986:22) said, Mach's approach determined much of Malinowski's anthropological work.

Whilst this is true, his approach to Mach's empiricism, positivism and monism was as cautious and critical as his reading of Frazer and Freud, as R. Thornton and P. Skalník, (1993:34) pointed out. This critical spirit, together with the desire to eliminate the conclusions of many of the theoretical systems against which he set his face was, without doubt, responsible for his extraordinary creative vision. Accepting Mach's belief that "theory creates fact", his openness to many theoretical perspectives enabled him to collect and observe a vast number of facts. Perhaps it should be remembered here that this phrase, "theory creates fact" appears in his *Diary* (Malinowski, 1967:114), but the same idea was expressed in his review of Frazer's book *Totemism and Exogamy* (p.127), in *Argonauts* (1922:84), in *Coral Gardens* (1935:317) and again in 1944 in his posthumous book *A Scientific Theory of Culture* (1944:12), where he wrote "to observe meanings in order to select, classify and isolate on the basis of theory".

For Mach, the objective of science was to describe phenomena concisely and economically. The best theory would also be the most economical one, that is, the theory which used the least possible number of variables. To describe a phenomenon in economical terms is to eliminate everything about it which appears unusual, and thus explain it. Description and explanation come to the same thing when explanation can be reduced to elemental sensations. Concepts and theories are provisional and economical tools to facilitate a mental representation of the facts. Theories are no more than perceptions of the world. This is what it means to speak metaphysically; to say that a theory is a painting which represents reality beyond appearances is to speak metaphysically, and does not respect the principle of the economy of thought. In order to make a phenomenon intelligible, we need to describe it solely in the terms with which we are familiar.

Apart from a philosophical critique of the arguments put forward by Averanius and Mach, other key elements which would continue to direct his thought appear in Malinowski's doctoral dissertation. Three aspects stand out:firstly, an attack on any temptation to reify abstract entities and anthropomorphise them, secondly, an epistemological and metaphysical concern with the nature of scientific truth in opposition to faith, and thirdly, an ontological concern with the closed nature of mental, physical and social systems and with the implications of this for a theory of change.

The first point addresses one of the hidden motives behind the dissertation. This hostility to the reification and humanisation of the abstract is especially evident in his rejection of the collective consciousness hypothesis put forward by Freud in *Totem and Taboo*, or of Durkheim and Rivers' belief in primitive communism. This concern would emerge repeatedly throughout his work.

Observations such as this were clearly stimulated not by positivism but by a deeper concern with metaphysics. But what did metaphysics really mean, for Malinowski? According to R. Thornton and P. Skalník, (1993:37), "at its worst, Malinowski understood metaphysics as an attempt to anthropomorphise the abstract structure of society, culture and the physical world. At its best, however, it meant a philosophical concern with the great contradictions and imponderables of life".

Lastly, and as Bestard observed in his introduction to Malinowski's brief essay (1995:26), in order to conduct a science of culture and respond to both the empirical principles in his dissertation and the questions regarding the nature of culture which had formed part of his years of training, Malinowski had to transform the study of culture, firstly by rejecting the possibility of historical knowledge as a basis for analysing cultural communities:meaning was to be found in the present, not the past, contrary to the precepts of evolutionary positivism. And secondly, by affirming that the totality of a culture was accessible to the present:cultural totalities formed entities containing elements which were functionally inter-related, contrary to romantic idealism. In order to achieve this, Malinowski had to locate himself beyond the course of history. He had to suppress both his personal history—culture is not individualistic, and his personal history could only be the subject of a personal journal—and its relationship to national history—culture is not national and national history was rather a question of political loyalties. Through its relationship with other cultures, culture could be seen as an ahistorical community rather than a community whose history had been rejected. The science of culture should be based on diversity rather than history, and experience became participant observation in a different cultural world. Modern anthropology emerged with the goal of empirically analysing cultural totalities, and Malinowski's Polish empiricism was one of the conditions for the appearance of this new theoretical object:the multiplicity of cultural totalities.

Religion and magic:*The Golden Bough* (1910?)

Malinowski's observations regarding Frazer's *The Golden Bough* are brief and undated, but almost certainly come from a long critical essay concerning Frazer's *Totemism and Exogamy* essay. Despite their brevity, his criticisms of Frazer's findings and conclusions are severe. It is also perhaps significant that, for the first time, he expressed some of the ideas which would later be more fully developed, above all in *Coral Gardens* (1935).

Malinowski criticised Frazer's psychology implicit in the 'principles of magic', claiming that this held close similarities to the psychology of Avenarius, which he had criticised earlier. Frazer had claimed that magic and science were similar in that magic implied a mode of reasoning about the material world which was no different in either kind or quality from that of science. Both magic and science were logical, and in so far as they were based on different assumptions, sought different kinds of conclusions. On this point, both science and magic differed from religion since the latter focused on a world of unseen forces and beings.

Malinowski's conclusions were significant because they implied a clear rupture with Frazer's intellectual approach and enabled him to initiate his own, more pragmatic approach. Considered as 'forms of thought', Malinowski claimed that magic and science were completely different. However, viewed as "human activity based on experience", they were "equivalent". Whilst science sought findings in terms of 'laws' which are more or less empirical, and defined its goals in terms of its findings, Malinowski believed that magic restricted its achievements to the rules of tradition and worship, defining its goals in terms of passion and desire. Thus, he did not distinguish between magic and science in terms of their 'contents', but rather in terms of the rules governing their use in a social context and defining their scope and use. Magic could be distinguished from science on the basis of how it was used and its purpose:the importance and purpose of both magic and science could only be decided in terms of their social context.

Therefore, whereas Frazer believed that magic and science were psychologically similar but sociologically different, Malinowski concluded the opposite, that they were psychologically different but similar in social practice. Frazer's error, according to R. Thornton and P. Skalník, (1993:40) resided in his focus on the psychological content of magic and science and his failure to consider either their use in context or their empirical forms.

Totemism and Exogamy (1911-1913)

Malinowski's critical review of *Totemism and Exogamy*, by Frazer, was published in three parts in the Polish journal *Lud*, between 1911 and 1913. Malinowski had already read and commented on *The Golden Bough*. He was now to evaluate the heuristic value of Frazer's work and the contribution made by all the material presented, and his criticism was strong and severe. He refuted Frazer's claims, theories and handling of his material. In brief, he felt that Frazer's proposals were a complete failure. Many of these criticisms were expressed orally in his classes at the LSE, but it is well known that on paper he restricted himself to praise of Frazer.

Malinowski argued that Frazer had misunderstood the mind of the savage, and criticised his tendency to assume that savages were 'utilitarian' and 'calculating'. Malinowski claimed that the Australians possessed myths, rather than 'interests' and calculations of utility, a crucial difference. He also criticised the fact that Frazer subordinated his descriptions to the scope provided by evolutionary theories, claiming that Frazer's attempt to organise his data according to this framework was a failure, given that the data used was insufficient to support the speculations made. He further criticised the intellectual distinction made between religion and magic, which prevented a theory of social change. Following Mach, he insisted that theories should consist of a description of the practical mechanisms or processes which show how change was produced, although always through empirical description.

Malinowski did not only criticise Frazer's methodology and other fundamental questions but also, as with his essays on Nietzsche or his dissertation on Mach, he used the material to formulate a series of questions and proposals for future empirical research. Among the most significant of the questions he raised was his attempt to see the rituals and beliefs of the Australians in terms of their 'economy'. Traditionally, Frazer and Durkheim had claimed that the Australians lacked economy, and it was precisely this lack which characterised them as primitive.

He also argued here, for the first time, that the family, not the horde, band, clan or any other larger unit, was the stable and elementary basis of social organisation, an aspect which he would develop further in his essay *Sociology of the Family* (1913-14), originally published in German and in *The Family Among the Australian Aborigines* (1913).

Here too he began to sketch out his own ideas regarding totemism, which he saw not so much as a belief or intellectual system as a form of social organisation. Malinowski introduced pragmatic criteria such as 'emotion' where Frazer simply considered 'logic', and he claimed that Frazer's definitions of magic and religion could not be empirically demonstrated since they belonged to the 'inner psychology of the native'.

The third section of Malinowski's critical review focused on a demolition of Frazer's theory of the origin of exogamy. Whilst Frazer considered that totemism and exogamy were parallel and comparable institutions, Malinowski distinguished between them on the basis that one, exogamy, was biological while the other, totemism, was 'constructed'.

More specifically, he considered Frazer's attempt to interpret social institutions as deriving from 'the logical consequence of belief' as erroneous. Malinowski insisted that a social institution should be explained in terms of the social conditions under which such institutions had developed. In other words, he said that totemism should be explained 'genetically', not 'logically'. Frazer's explanation of totemism in terms of its speculative origins "does not give the genesis of totemic beliefs, much less the genesis of totemic social institutions". Malinowski's criticism was also directed against Frazer's interest in 'origins', a notion that Malinowski ridiculed, just as he did Frazer's conception of history, which Malinowski considered inadequate for a rigorous understanding of the data.

Tribal masculine associations in Australia (1912)

This essay, published in both Polish and English, was one of the first examples of Malinowski's application of functionalism. His rejection of evolution was stronger and even more explicit, and he repeated his attack on the notion of 'origins'. The aim of the essay was to demonstrate that one particular institution, the secret male society, served the function of creating and maintaining social power based on the categories of age and gender, and that its mythical nature justified these practices and beliefs. Malinowski fluctuated between the original ethnological questions about the position of entire societies, tribes or peoples on the scale of evolution, complexity or political maturity, and new concerns such as the relationships between institutions in a single functioning society.

He gave a brief summary of aspects of Australian kinship, economy and sexuality, mentioning male homosexuality and the extensive privileges of elder males. He also pointed out the distinction between exogamous marriage classes and totemic clans and the fundamental role of initiation ceremonies. Through the evidence he presented, he showed how these institutions acted to exclude women from public life, ensure separation on the basis of class, age and sex, and reinforce a strict hierarchy regulating access to goods and prestige.

He used their myths to illustrate his approach and once again attack the question of an interest in origins. From the point of view of the native, myths seek to show how, and not why or when, these practices were introduced.

The idea that gender and power were culturally constructed through myths, and socially instituted through concrete ritual practices underlay his arguments. Karl Parson, Havelock Ellis and Freud had already published works making similar claims which, according to Stocking (1986), were known to Malinowski, although he only cited Parson. These propositions marked a new direction and anticipated his book *The sexual life of savages* (1929).

Economic aspects of the Intichiuma ceremonies (1912)

In this essay, Malinowski attempted to develop further the economic aspects of totemism that he had formulated in his criticism of Frazer's *Totemism and exogamy*. At the end of that critical review, and also in *The relation of primitive beliefs to forms of social organisation*, he had asserted that totemism was as much an economic as a religious phenomenon. Now, in developing these ideas further in this essay, he drew on those of the economist and historian Karl Bücher, with whom he had studied in Leipzig between 1909 and 1910.

According to R. Thornton and P. Skalník, (1993:52), Malinowski appears to have followed Bücher's definition of 'work', which enabled him to understand the activities of the Australian Aborigines in broadly comparative terms, rather than in strictly evolutionist terms. Bücher noted the temporal rhythm and periodicity of work in an industrial society, and demonstrated how the temporal division of the day and the discipline of time were at least as important as the division of tasks, what he called the 'division of labour'.

Herbert Spencer, James Frazer and Emile Durkheim considered specialised labour and the division of tasks as characteristic of industrialised societies. In this essay, however, Malinowski was to demonstrate something different. The *Intichiuma* ritual, through which *Arunta* increased and fertilised the natural species associated with their *totems*, was a complex institution:a social, public obligation founded in myth, and with religious rather than magical laws. It presented multiple functions which provoked the following three questions:1) in what sense is *Intichiuma* economic? 2) if it is, is there a functional connection between economy and magic? and, 3) is this connection necessary or merely accidental? The essay's title provided the answer. It was economic, but not in a sterile sense, but in a more productive sense. These ceremonies required "collective work organised by the community", and "demanded a considerable amount of work, carried out with great care and with a complete awareness of their importance", they were regular and periodic, and were consciously aimed at the goal of "increasing totemic animals and plants". Furthermore, the magic was used to attain economic goals. "Whether they attain them or not is of no importance to the native, who only pursues the material results of these practices".

Thus, Malinowski concluded that totemism represented more than a false description of reality in terms of identifying clans with their totemic species, and that it was rather a practice and form of social organisation which motivated and trained the people for the work required to achieve specific goals. Although such goals were mythological, their effects were practical. Magic, used by the native due to a belief in its effectiveness, could be understood in Frazer's terms, as an 'intellectual error', or as a practical and economic technique. Thus the economic functions of religion and magical ideas became a new subject for inquiry. All these ideas were later developed in *Coral Gardens*, where he wrote "the two ways, the way of magic and the way of garden work—*megara la kada, bagual la kada*—are inseparable. They are never confused, nor is one of them ever allowed to supercede the other (. . .) nor does this distinction between work and magic remain implicit and unexpressed (Malinowski, 1935, I:76-77).

Once again, in this essay he rejected "any universal evolutionist schema" and declared his support for an approach which addressed "economic evolution . . . separately, contextualised in each ethnographic area and according to the specific conditions of each of them". I will return to this theme later on, when I discuss his contributions to the study of economics.

A fundamental problem in the sociology of religion (1914)

The previous conclusion about totemism in reference to economics generated a new problem which Malinowski developed further in this brief essay on Durkheim's definition of religion. If the *Intichiuma* ceremonies were both religious and economic, then their sacredness made sense if religion was defined in terms of a dichotomy between sacred and profane, as Durkheim had done. But Malinowski considered that the distinction between sacred and profound was merely a social and contextual aspect of Australian religion in particular, and thus without general theoretical consequences.

The relationship of primitive beliefs to the forms of social organisation (1913)

In this essay, Malinowski took as his starting point a question which he had left unanswered at the end of his critique of Frazer's *Totemism and Exogamy*. In an explicit attempt to clearly formulate a concept and articulate a method, he showed that totemism did not exist as a category of concepts or practices, nor was it an institution which could exist throughout different historical periods, cultures and societies. At most, totemism was a series of heterogeneous phenomena, some of which were 'social' whilst others were 'religious'. In other words, totemism did not have a simply defined or 'unequivocally determined' *essence*.

Malinowski argued that totemism was a 'social' phenomenon which was closely related to a specific form of social organisation, and that its purpose was to unite the clan with the tribal unit. In this, Malinowski coincided with Durkheim but remained outside the evolutionist framework. In other words, he did not consider totemism a "primitive form of science" but rather an "attitude towards the environment". This attitude, he said, was complex, and was conditioned but not determined by "the struggle for existence", a lack of control over natural events, changes produced by life crises and sexuality, and the need for protection and defence against "real and imaginary" danger.

Malinowski also agreed with Durkheim in that the idea of totemism was not related to individual animals but rather to categories of animals, comparable to species. They also coincided in the logical status of totemism, which appeared both as a natural classification and a categorical imperative, providing a theory of natural order for the environment and moral order for society. To a certain extent, all these ideas anticipated the work of Claude Lévi-Strauss, as R. Thornton and P. Skalník indicated (1993:60).

The Sociology of the Family (1913-1914)

This essay, written in German, is considered his weakest in terms of its theoretical basis. It is divided into two parts. In the first, Malinowski briefly reviewed the literature on the evolution of kinship, focusing on Maine, Fustel de Coulanges, Grote, Bachofen, Morgan and McLennan, on other, less well-known authors such as Hildeabrand, Dargun and Muller-Lyer, and also on others whom he knew because they had carried out their work in Krakow and Leipzig, where he himself had studied.

In the second section, he also dealt briefly with contemporary studies (that is, research which had been conducted around 1913) of the sociology of the American and European family, and the problems he faced and had attempted to change. This review reflects the intense and widespread interest in Europe in the 'problem' of women, children, sex—especially in terms of the institution of marriage—child labour, prostitution and the exclusion of women from political life. All these issues provoked intense debate among trade unionists, politicians, intellectuals and artists, etc., but not in the field of ethnography. This essay reveals a deep knowledge of the literature on the question, which Malinowski reviewed, and constitutes a precursor to the first book he wrote in English, *The Family among the Australian Aborigines*, published in 1913.

Bearing in mind that most of the sociological literature at the time was written for journals, or in the service of a particular ideology, religion or political standpoint, Malinowski did not see a new way of understanding these problems other than by maintaining a distance from them. He suggested that this failure was due to the fact that ethnologists were too close to the data on their own society to understand them well. Thus, he pointed to the horizons of field work and expeditions to other societies where, since the data was further from personal experience, they could be viewed more clearly,

All these early works represented a period of intense theoretical production prior to his departure for New Guinea. They were written from a perspective that he would later criticise harshly, since in their writing he had used sources which had not always been compiled by professionals. His constant rejection of evolutionist theories due to their conjectural and speculative nature, gives these essays a repetitive and monotonous character, although this would later serve him as the basis for developing his new paradigm, presented in later works.

2. MALINOWSKI'S ORIGINAL CONTRIBUTIONS

Malinowski's initial contributions appear in his critiques of the theories put forward by earlier authors, as we have seen in the foregoing section. In the first monographs that he wrote following his field work, he began to introduce a series of concepts and ideas which, through a process of continuous reformulation, he continued to adapt until reaching his final theoretical stance. I will now examine this process through a study of his first monographs.

2.1. Malinowski's first monographs

The Family among the Australian Aborigines, published in 1913, can be considered Malinowski's first monograph, although this is not strictly true since this study of Australian aborigines was not the product of research conducted *in situ* by Malinowski himself, but was rather a compilation of well-documented observations. Panoff (1974:23 and ss.) wrote that this book exudes an aroma of "mustiness", although it also presents "refreshing virtues". In general, the monograph is not held in high esteem by scholars. Whilst in general, the universe of the Australian aborigines evokes an exceedingly complex sociology of matrimonial systems and is an inexhaustible source of reflection on the theory of 'totemism', and more generally on 'primitive thought', subjects which were extensively addressed subsequently by authors from Radcliffe-Brown to Lévi-Strauss, Malinowski did not refer to either one or the other of these questions, an omission which no small number of his colleagues have commented on.

It is nevertheless true that through this book, published in the second decade of the 20th century, Malinowski (1913:300-302) portrayed himself as the only one to appoint himself the task of defining and studying the conjugal family (or 'nuclear family' as it is known today) since, due to reasons stemming from the ideology of the times, the majority of theoreticians were reluctant to believe that it was possible, among such 'backward' subjects as the Australian aborigines, for an institution to exist which was based on individual bonds between a man, a woman and their progeny. Generalised sexual promiscuity or tribal communities seemed much more plausible. Even Durkheim felt incapable of imagining an Australian conjugal family in any way other than as the coupling of a male and female in order to ensure reproduction. Today, it is still interesting to refer to Malinowski's approach to these questions.

The exclusive attention paid to the conjugal family in this study has its drawbacks:the family was presented by Malinowski as isolated from the rest of the group, and relationships with other groups in indigenous society (kin, horde) were conspicuously neglected. This was a lapse for which he was repeatedly criticised when he published the study:however, by limiting his focus he was able to hand down to his successors some important principles which have become the ABC of kinship studies. Firstly, his hostility to Morgan led him to clarify the concept of 'kinship' and 'consanguinity' (Malinowski, 1913:171 and 200) and to establish a distinction between biological and sociological kinship (*Ibíd.*:176-179). In fact, Malinowski asserted that the relationship between individuals and their descendents, as verified through procreation ('biological kinship'), was of no interest to the anthropologist (*Ibíd.*:177), and any attempt to identify it as the nexus of kinship sanctioned by society, simply because in our society the two usually coincide, was tantamount to prohibiting the study of exotic societies. However, this became a basic rule on which modern anthropology was founded, and on which Malinowski himself would make a brilliant contribution in *The Father in Primitive Psycology* (1927), illustrating the specific problems posed by matrilineal societies.

Secondly, Malinowski introduced a discussion, albeit brief, on the concept of 'descent' (Malinowski, 1913:184). In this instance, his definition has not only stood the test of time posed by technical refinements introduced subsequently into the discipline, but his demand that when speaking of descent, the exact group referred to from among the various levels (residential unit, clan, phratry) should be specified, remains pertinent today. Modern anthropology does not take the rule of descent as the essential focus of kinship studies:rather, matrimony, place of residence, adoption, etc., are the subjects of greater attention both on the part of theoreticians and of observers.

In *The Family among the Australian Aborigines* (1913), Malinowski advocated a very limited stance as regards the role of descent, and minimised its importance, not because he felt that other aspects of the social structure were of equal or greater importance, as many ethnographers do today, but because, for him, the parent-child bond was essentially based on affection and emotion. Consequently, he placed more emphasis on individual spontaneity and, more generally, on the factors inherent in individual psychology. From the first to the last page of the book, Malinowski's purpose was to separate the subject of study, the nuclear family, from more formal superstructures, particularly those of a judicial nature.

This desire to advocate the primacy of affection and spontaneity led him to establish a distinction between descent and procreation, and to clarify the concepts of law and judicial rules in terms which would be applicable to a diversity of cultures. Malinowski's successors, however, did not continue in this vein and these proposals were abandoned due to the influence of Radcliffe-Brown:modern ethology would be aimed more at seeking explicit correlations between phenomena. In contrast, the theory according to which the nuclear or conjugal family should be considered the centre of the sociological universe of kinship has continued to inspire the analyses conducted by modern theoreticians (for example, Murdock and Lounsbury, among others).

The second monograph, ***The Natives of Mailu,*** published in 1915, is an ethnographic description of the natives amongst whom he lived for various months at the start of his period in New Guinea. It cannot be said that this book marks a milestone in his career, but it is nevertheless of interest since it was the first to emerge from his own field work.

In his introduction to the book, Michael Young (1988:24) wrote that it was essentially a field report of the sort that Haddon or Seligman had produced. In the book,

Malinowski examined many of the visible, and some of the less visible aspects of the *Mailu* culture. It does not have the textual richness of his best monographs on the Trobriand Islands, but it does contain topics of equal interest which emerged as the result of following, fairly slavishly if not to the letter, the format given in *Notes and Queries on Anthropology*, published by Rivers in 1905 for the *Royal Anthropological Institute*.

There is no institutional focus or thematic unity to the monograph, nor did Malinowski narrate a story as he was to do in later works, where a previous design already existed. But the influence of the fourth edition of *Notes and Queries* on the textual structure of *Mailu* is persistent and easy to demonstrate. Malinowski took a copy of the book with him on his three expeditions, and he himself referred to the book in his monograph (Malinwoksi, 1915:110). Furthermore, he cited it occasionally in his *Diary* (Malinowski, 1967).

The systematic division of the chapters ("Geography", "Sociology", "Economy", "Magical and religious activities and beliefs", etc.) permits a straightforward comparison with the typical organisation used in *Notes and Queries*. The main points in chapter II of *Mailu*, "Social Division", are taken from the section "Social Organisation" written by Rivers. Chapter III, "Tribal Life", represents a further development of section I, "Daily Life". It begins with a "division of the day", but recalls the section on sleep, hygiene, dress, cleanliness, food preparation, cooking, narcotics, etc., following the *Notes and Queries* "Technology" categories closely. Section 5 of this chapter, on "Legal Institutions" is based on the chapter entitled "Government:Politics". And so on. In all the chapters and sections in *Mailu*, we find a correlation with the parts comprising *Notes and Queries*, although regrouped for his own purposes.

It appears that three of Malinowski's four or five original notebooks on the *Mailu* have survived, handwritten in reasonably legible English, with *Mailu* nouns and words written in capital letters. M. Young (1988:27) has asserted that it is enlightening to examine these in order to understand how Malinowski composed the monograph. In particular, his field notes are reasonably consistent with the monograph he later produced in his study, and the two correlate fairly well. This does not invalidate later assertions by Malinowski concerning the "enormous distance between raw material in the form of collected data, and the final presentation of results" (Malinowski, 1922:3-4), but rather demonstrates that in the case of the *Mailu* monograph, at least, the distance was shorter. To the extent that *Mailu* was written as a 'compendium of ethnographic facts', reproduced directly from the author's note books, we can deduce that writing it was easy. It appears that he transcribed entire pages, making only small, essential changes in the final draft. The logical consequence was that the intellectual task was less burdensome, and the time necessary to write the monograph accordingly shorter. However, it is also true that the monograph refers to questions which did not present many problems and were generally related to practical or technological issues, such as personal adornment, canoe building, dances, crop growing, etc. This was not always the case, and certain subjects received more attention, for instance topics related to law, taboo, land holding, feasts and other subjects which he needed to fit into his theoretical and discursive framework. These were social facts of a different order. Thus, Malinowski's sections on complex institutional structures are the longest, and the best theoretically documented. Here, it is more difficult to deduce how they were written based solely on his field notes, and it is surprising to find that these subjects are spread throughout all the notebooks, suggesting that he returned to them time and time again, whenever he had the opportunity. Nevertheless, much of the text is mere technical description, presented together with his own diagrams and photographs.

A comparison with *Argonauts of the Western Pacific* (1922) is unnecessary but inevitable. Historically speaking, if *Argonauts* is a window on the future (post-1922), *Natives of Mailu* is a window on the past (pre-1915). As is well-known, it was from *Argonauts* onwards that Malinowski began to declare his *revolution*:radical changes in field ethnography, and equally radical changes in the way ethnography was written.

Baloma:the Spirit of the Dead in the Trobriand Islands, published in 1916, is a further instance. It was his first work on the natives of the Trobriand Islands, and it is where Malinowski's attitude to the world of thought is clearly revealed, in a foreign environment in which he would live for much longer than any other anthropologist had ever done before. In addition, it was also written in the narrative style for which his best work is famous:a fundamental sensitivity and a constant concern for the concrete which slowly lends coherence and intelligibility to the entire sphere of reality addressed, offering the reader the possibility of following even those ramifications most distant from the initial observations. Although this might not be the most fundamental feature, in general it does represent a more scientific spirit. Throughout his presentation of the facts, Malinowski also included a series of subjective notes about his personal contact with the Melanesians (Panoff, 1974:29).

The entire article is centred on the question of beliefs and representations related to the soul and the hereafter among the inhabitants of the Trobriand Islands. Research carried out previously had shown Malinowski that the social activities related to the phenomenon of death, such as rules governing mourning and funeral rites, constituted a separate reality, the study of which could not be undertaken before conducting a complete analysis of aboriginal society. But all these observations are merely marginal, as the principal interest of the study, written after three months of intensive data collection, resides in his detailed presentation of previously unknown facts, and in his discussion of divergent information. On the one hand, the natives of the Trobiand Islands believed in the existence of two kinds of soul:*baloma*, which was the main and lasting form of the deceased's spirit, and *kosi*, an ill-defined and hazy entity, with a short and fleeting life span in the places that the deceased used to frequent in life. The former would go to stay definitively on the Island of the Spirits, whereas the latter was characterised by terrorising the living in the days following the demise. The problem that Malinowski attempted to solve was the relationship between these two kinds of soul, and how the natives explained their coexistence during life and after death. Therefore, he studied the metaphors which emerged repeatedly when speaking of the two entities (*Baloma* was likened to the reflection of a human being in a mirror, whilst *kosi* was likened to a human's shadow), the different behaviours attributed to them and the bonds which could retain them in the bodies of the living. But he failed to establish a coherent theory which explained this duality. Malinowski reached the conclusion that the two sets of beliefs had similar credibility and that neither was more orthodox than the other, which gave him the opportunity to present several hypotheses on the nature and function of religious and magical thought in their relationship to the demands of rational thought, and to show how, within the framework of a dogmatism which evaded all contradiction, individuals freely improvised 'theological' explanations which were as adroit as they were easily relegated to oblivion shortly afterwards.

On the other hand, and despite the evident divergences reported by his informants, there was unanimous agreement regarding the most fundamental belief, which asserted that pregnancy was the consequence of an incursion on the uterus by a spirit which had abandoned the kingdom of the dead to recommence a new life in the world of the living. No child could come into the world without the prior intervention of one of the mother's ancestors, who would provide the life force, and the role of the father in the biological mechanism of procreation was completely unacknowledged. Ignorance concerning the process of fertilisation, whilst at the same time insistence on the part of his informants that coitus was the *sine qua non* condition of pregnancy, such was the apparent contradiction present in the testimonies Malinowski compiled.

The final part of the article is a 'methodological' essay about *in situ* research. Here, Malinowski examined the problem of obtaining and interpreting the ethnographic data referred to in his report, and proposed a goal as apparently modest as the ethnographic description which preceded it:to present facts, nothing more than facts—on this occasion, however, with the aim of selecting and annotating the results of the observations in a scientifically useful form. In other words, the substance of this conclusion consisted of the epistemological difficulties inherent in the act of observing and describing exotic institutions, and of the manner in which he overcame them. Before leading us to the 'terrain', he teaches us that we should collect the raw facts and guard them carefully from contamination by any other interpretation:it was in these terms that

Malinowski (1916:237-238) introduced his subject, and he continued, "facts do not exist in the emotional world; only the immediate emergence of chaos exists. 'Facts' are always the work of intellectuals, the consequence of an inevitable decision to select, isolate, generalise, etc.'. To summarise, facts only existed in their raw state, but always implied selection by the researcher.

He acknowledged the attention that should be paid to the 'social dimension' (íbid:239) as the driving force behind the research process ("a belief does not exist as a scientific fact, but rather is understood in its 'social dimension' "), and remarked on the problem of relating the reports by informants to the status these held individually within their society, and of contrasting the beliefs and opinions of various individuals with the practices sanctioned by the culture within the framework of one or another institution:it would be necessary to evaluate the data collected and take stock of the setting. Information should be collected establishing distinctions between three kinds of opinion:explanations codified by tradition and only available from experts; general opinions formulated by the majority of the members of the community, and, lastly, individual speculations proffered by certain informants endowed with more intelligence than the norm. The next stage would consist in clarification, through comparison, of the information collected. Thus, the problem resided in selection of informants, the form of conduct due to them according to their social status and the commentary of their testimonies. Few texts offer so much useful advice in so few words to someone preparing to work in the field for the first time.

Structurally and stylistically, Malinowski's essay on *Baloma* represents a transition between the previous essay on the *Natives of Mailu* and his later work, *Argonauts*. A reading of all three reveals his growing maturity and a stylistic change over the six years which had passed between the former and the latter, and shows how he assayed a style in the first two that would be embodied in the third, which became a seminal work.

3. ECONOMIC ANTHROPOLOGY AND THE ANTHROPOLOGY OF RELIGION:FROM *ARGONAUTS* TO *CORAL GARDENS AND THEIR MAGIC*

Between 1920 and the end of the 30s, whilst he was teaching at the London School of Economics, Malinowski published a series of articles and monographs which reflected his intellectual and scientific maturity. All were based on to his field work carried out on the Trobriand Islands, and through them he developed his functionalist approach to cultural analysis. Thus, he wrote *Argonauts of the Western Pacific* (1922), *The Sexual Life of Savages in North-Western Melanesia* (1929) and *Coral Gardens and their Magic:A Study of the Methods of Tilling the Soil and of Agricultural Rites in the Trobriand Islands* (1935), three of the most important ethnographic monographs of all time. He also published a series of articles which supported and complemented his arguments and contributions in practically all areas of the discipline of anthropology.

Malinowski did not give a systematic presentation of the various aspects he studied, but rather, from his holistic approach to culture as functional units, he generally returned to the same aspects throughout his entire works. It is for this reason that in order to conduct a systematic review of his contribution it is necessary to refer to practically his entire oeuvre, throughout which we always find something new due to this latent reiteration even though his approach to different contexts displayed little variation or evolution, to the extent that on several subjects he remained as hesitant at the end as he was at first.

In order to explore the most noteworthy aspects of his work, such as economics, magic and religion, or his approach to subjects related to psychology and linguistics, I will focus, in an attempt at synthesis, on the works in which this contribution is clearest and most evident.

3.1. *Argonauts* and Economic Anthropology.

In 1922, Malinowski published **Argonauts of the Western Pacific**, one of his greatest works and also one of the most important books in the history of ethnographic literature. Two aspects indicate that this was a significant and original book:on the one hand, it established a new approach to intellectual and emotional experience, which was its starting point, and on the other, the manner in which Malinowski articulated the different elements which were the result of his observations. Although Malinowski, as we have seen, was not the first to study societies *in situ*, he did introduce an innovation as regards the methods that until then had been applied, by spending more than two years of his life on the Melanesian archipelago. Two years which he spent severed from Europeans and in contact only with the natives. In order to participate more fully in their lives, he made the effort to learn their language. This was another, and more crucial, innovation (Panoff, 1974:35). Until then, whenever an ethnographer used the vernacular, it was to record mythological texts or rituals, dictated by an expert informant. From this moment onwards, ethnographers stopped relying entirely on privileged informants and sought to communicate with all members of the society Consequently, the nature of the material compiled was also transformed:it no longer consisted of texts or traditions frozen in time, but rather the totality of social life came under scrutiny. These conditions, which Malinowski applied during his field work, shaped the argument of the book and its radical originality rendered it a study without precedent. Furthermore, Malinowski appears as a great teacher, clearly explaining his goals, he had wished to carry out and his *modus operandi*, and above all in his critique of earlier scientific descriptions and the subjective accounts of amateurs, whether travellers, traders or missionaries.

The subject matter of *Argonauts*, trade between the tribes of the Massim region to the south east of New Guinea, was not strictly new:similar institutions in the Samoan Islands, in New Caledonia and closer to the Trobriand Islands, in Papua, had already been mentioned and even described. However, what did appear for the first time was a description by an ethnographer of how a particular institution functioned, including observations on all its ramifications across all levels of social reality. According to the approach proposed by Malinowski in his book, the ritual exchange, or the *kula*, of certain precious objects, or *vaygu'a*, which formed the principal subject matter of the book, could not be understood without extensive reference to native technology (navigation, fishing, the use of shell currency), the existing hierarchical system, the ideology of honour and of generosity, the mythology and magic. Thus, he attempted to demonstrate that it was impossible to make sense of social facts unless they were considered from the perspective of their location inside the totality of a particular society's set of institutions (from here, Marcel Mauss would take the ideas he developed in his essay *The Gift*, and in particular, the concept of a 'total social fact').

I will provide a brief synthesis of the most characteristic features of *Argonauts*, necessary in order to contextualise those aspects to which I refer. The complex institution described, called the *kula*, consisted of an inter-tribal system of exchange which covered over 150,000 square kilometres and included thousands of natives spread over twenty different islands. It could not be described as trade since the transactions were not based on merchandise which satisfied material needs but on objects "completely devoid of any utility and very similar as regards their possible function to the Crown Jewels" (Malinowski, 1922:95-103).

There were only two kinds of object, shell armbands and necklaces. They were never withdrawn from the circuit, or the *kula ring*, and were exchanged from island to island, community to community and even house to house, following an invariable route over the entire trading circuit:the red shell necklaces, or *soulava*, were always traded in a clockwise direction whereas the white shell armbands, or *mwali*, were circulated in an anti-clockwise direction (see map in Figure 2). Passed from hand to hand after long journeys, whether by sea or on foot, the objects took between two and ten years to complete the circuit and return to their point of departure. Although the islanders were intent on receiving, in the more or less long term, as much as they gave, bartering was rigorously prohibited, and any islander who attempted it would be irremediably discredited. At the same time as these 'noble' exchanges took place, other trading operations were carried out of a lucrative and utilitarian nature. However, these were differentiated and separate from the *kula ring*, to the extent that the worst possible insult that could be offered was to accuse a man of trading the former as if it were the latter. *Kula* exchange between two partners involved them in obligations of reciprocal hospitality, protection and, in times of war, assistance, and they would be united in friendship.

Figure 2: The Kula Ring.

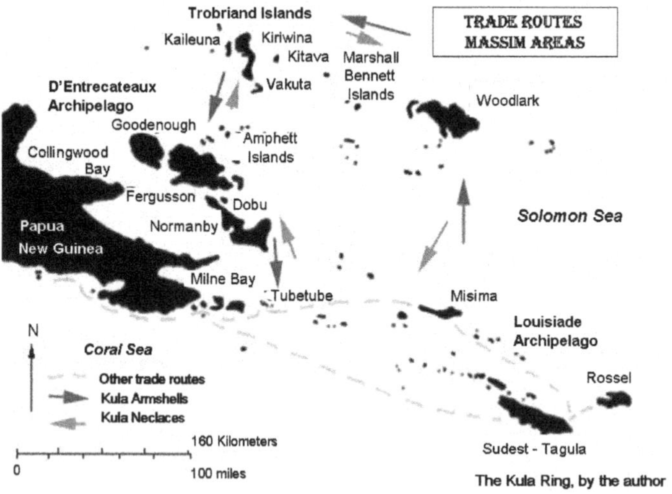

The Kula Ring, by the author

Due to the ritual nature of *kula* exchange and the particular bonds which united *kula* partners, not all the inhabitants of the Trobriand Islands and the other islands included in the circuit participated in this vast operation.

In each of the tribes, a more or less limited number of individuals had the right to give or receive ceremonial armbands and necklaces. This did not mean that this was a privilege reserved exclusively for chiefs, as Marcel Mauss for example understood, as evidenced in his essay *The Gift*. No individual was excluded from this trade, but less influential individuals would have fewer exchange partners, and the exchange they carried out would be less complex and also less prestigious.

The system was based on two different but complementary forms of exchange. The first involved long sea expeditions to transport prodigious quantities of precious objects, and this form provides the most conspicuous, but not the only, image of the institution. The second, much less ceremonial form, involved repeated exchanges between owners over a distance of no more than a few kilometres (inland *kula*). Each of these two forms led to an infinite series of collective activities which, although secondary to the ultimate purpose of the institution, played a crucially important economic role through the mobilisation of a variety of resources for the feasts offered in honour of the *kula* visitors, the construction of large canoes and the production and trade of articles unavailable on some of the islands involved in the circuit, etc.

As regards social life on the Trobriand Islands, the system revolved around three figures:the chief, the sorcerer and the garden magician. Chiefdom was the institution which gave the Melanesian society its distinctive character, but the study of magic was no less important and Malinowski dedicated a quarter of his book to this subject. The stratification of society and the regulation of employment arising from an excess of production formed the two most important manifestations of the role played by a chief on the Trobriand Islands. The 'chief' based his authority on two aspects:his acknowledged preeminence conceded on the grounds of his individual qualities, and his membership of a high-ranking clan in the kinship group hierarchy However, the power and prestige enjoyed by the highest-ranking chiefs did not exempt them from the obligation to provide remuneration for the labour they demanded from workers and for the displays of loyalty that these gave. Chiefdom was closely related to a plutocratic organisation. Nevertheless, the wealth that a chief should have at his disposal in order to maintain his rank came for the most part from his in-laws, clearly and immediately indicating the great economic importance of polygamy, a practice reserved for high-ranking individuals. However, this wealth, without which the chief would be nobody, sooner or later would be returned to the community of which he was the chief. This leads us to the second economic aspect of Trobriand Island chiefdom:in addition to the role that the chiefs played in regulating the production process, they also functioned as a mechanism for centralisation and distribution of the available surplus. This explains why all individuals were obliged to present the chief with three quarters of their harvest, a proportion which might seem enormous and yet was not when one becomes aware of the system governing the circulation of goods within the society. A schematic representation of this system is given in Figure 3.

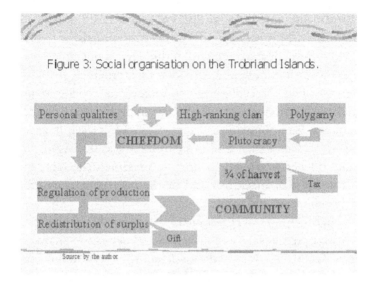

Figure 3: Social organisation on the Trobriand Islands.

Source: by the author

Of equal importance for cultural continuity and cohesion on the Trobriand Islands, although not of an economic nature, was the existence of a special kind of magic and its transmission over generations of a body of nautical knowledge and techniques which also formed part of the system of ritual *kula* exchange. Thanks to Malinowski's keen observations, there is such an extraordinary wealth of facts described in *Argonauts* that he contrived to communicate their grandeur and render us fellow travellers on his journey through the *kula* system. Moreover, in order to enable us to follow his footsteps, he provided successive descriptions over the different chapters, as if narrating a story, of the construction of canoes, the preparations for the journey, the ceremonies prior to departure, the crossing, etc.

Returning to questions of an economic nature, these form the central focus of the book in two respects, both as regards the reflections they elicit in the reader and in terms of the insights and actions of the author himself. The initial fundamental questions are "what is economics?" and "does anything which corresponds to this concept exist in other civilisations outside our own?" Although it is not altogether clear what Malinowski understood by economics, perhaps because of his scant education as a 'professional economist' or perhaps due to his lack of knowledge of the literature on the subject, his response to these questions reveals the influence (as mentioned earlier and as he himself acknowledged) of Karl Bücher, above all in how he presented the facts in his analysis of incentives and of the parallel relationship between magic and work.

In his critique of evolutionary theses, and based on these negative premises, he established a series of positive analyses to redress these errors, and thus demonstrated the following points, as summarised by Firth (1974 b:228):

1. The supposition that in their economic affairs, primitive people are exclusively rational, utilitarian and logical is a serious error:social interests, social restrictions and the emerging social structure dictate much of the economic behaviour of savages.

2. Since there is evidence of economic organisation among the Australian aborigines, the Mailu and the Trobriand Islanders, it is unlikely that there are any contemporary primitive peoples to be found who exist in a pre-economic state (as Bücher established).

3. Far from being indolent, individualistic and selfish, and irresponsible in their economic affairs, the 'savage' is capable of carrying out sustained hard work.

4. Contrary to popular belief, 'savages' are very organised and systematic in their approach to work.

5. By no means are trade and exchange in primitive communities necessarily rudimentary. Rather, they can be regular, organised and complex both as regards the operations involved and the stimuli they imply.

6. Primitive concepts of property cannot be defined either by group 'communism' or by exclusively individual rights to possession, but rather in terms of multiple rights exercised by groups and individuals.

All these generalisations, which today seem obvious, were of great importance in their day, when the dominant conceptual philosophy was that of a rigid evolutionism which impeded a rigorous analysis of behaviour.

As his work progressed, his conceptualisation of the problem broadened and became closer to modern approaches. He never presented his material on the Trobriand Islands as a complete and ordered account of the economic system, but rather described the system from the perspective of its intimate relationship with the social structure which gave it meaning and which it reinforced. Thus, in his early writings, specifically those which examined work as an economic aspect of the *Intichiuma* ceremonies (Malinowksi, 1912), when he was still preoccupied with the evolutionist theses of Bücher, he attempted to relate the economy and economic work to the type of work carried out in civilised industrial companies. The difference did not reside in the quantity of work carried out, but in its nature. In order for it to be called economic, it should be "sustained, periodically repeated and planned rationally". Malinowski even asserted that "primitive work was completely ineffectual for economic purposes" (1912:224). But he contributed to an analysis of the anthropological concept of work, and indicated the role of totemism as an economic incentive, in contrast to Frazer, who had claimed that the principle economic function of totemism was to give rise to a rudimentary division of labour, although such as function was of little importance in totemism. For his part, Malinowski demonstrated that in the context of totemism, work did have an important economic function, for example the way in which the *Intichiuma* ceremonies fostered economic goals, particularly arduous collective labour of an organised kind. To summarise, his entire argument revolved around the assertion that "in order to explain the training of men in economic activity, it is necessary to take into account the idea of magical and religious ideas as coercive mental forces" (Malinowksi, 1912:210).

His publication *The family among the Australian aborigines* (Malinowski, 1913) included several topics which were to appear repeatedly in his later treatment of economic aspects. He examined property rights, the division of labour, including division based on sex, and the economics of the individual family, thus explicitly relating social structure and economic organisation. He posed questions such as "To what extent did the individual family in Australia constitute an economic unit?", and "How do economic facts determine the individuality of a particular family?" and responded by asserting that it was precisely the division of labour in the home which established the unity of the social group from an economic point of view.

His ethnographic report on the Mailu (1915) also contains some material of interest regarding economics. He examined the 'agricultural laws' of the Mailu regarding property and also gave data on the use and ownership of canoes, fishing, etc., together with other complementary details. Although brief, highly specific and relatively unsystematic, the report gave a clear indication of the direction his subsequent analytical treatment was to take, for example that the principle psychological element in ownership of hunting land, or of nets or canoes "appears to be more the desire for social pre-eminence than the desire for a greater share of material goods", or that the natives placed great value on the right to give things as presents or to concede to others the use of their own privileges (Malinowski, 1915:254 and ss.).

As Firth points out (1974 b:234), from this point onwards Malinowski's approach developed in two directions. One was a detailed analysis of the economic data from the Trobriand Islands in relation to the social data, and the results of this appeared in his analysis of the *kula ring* and of the agriculture of the Trobriand Islanders (Malinowski, 1922, 1935). The other direction was a more general examination of the role of economic organisation in social and cultural life, a subject which Malinowski developed as part of his general analysis of culture (Malinowski, 1931).

Malinowski suggested that economic behaviour was part of the overall system of social behaviour. He realised that the way in which a community utilised their resources reflected a crucial set of data for scientific study, data which were interesting in themselves but even more so in relation to the social activities from which they could only be separated conceptually. One of the most important aspects of his studies was the development of his ideas on the role of economics in relation to magic. In his study of the Mailu, he demonstrated that the mgical rituals related to hunting and agriculture were clearly considered to be endowed with economic value, and he was able to document this later on the Trobriand Islands. As Firth indicates (1974 b:235), in his first general analysis of the Trobriand economy, Malinowski also provided a succinct outline of the role of the garden magician:by supervising activities of general importance, such as enclosing the gardens, this public servant provided a direct stimulus to production. Indirectly, he contributed to production in four different ways:by taking the initiative in starting work on the gardens; by regulating the pace of work and inaugurating the successive phases; by establishing standards of quality in certain key gardens, for magical purposes, through monitoring; and, lastly, by imposing taboos, which were the equivalent of specific sanctions regarding working practice. In his analysis of the *kula*, Malinowski broadened this description to indicate that these were all positive productive functions. To summarise, it is to Malinowski that we owe the introduction into economic anthropological debate of magic as an economic entity, a factor in production or service and as a product or object of economic value.

Malinowski's constant awareness of the social context and of the importance of factors such as compliance with ritual obligations led him to criticise the concept of 'Primitive Economic Man' harshly. In *Argonauts* (1922:74 and ss.), he compared what he called "this fantastic and fictitious creature, which has led a tenacious existence in popular and semi-popular literature, and whose shadow obsesses even competent anthropologists" with the Trobriand Islanders of flesh and blood whom he knew. He severely critisised the idea of a primitive man "motivated in all his actions by a rational idea of self-interest" and argued that just one well-established example would suffice to show how ridiculous this assumption was. In this respect, Malinowski helped those working in these marginal areas to classify the distinction between 'homo oeconomicus', constructed by economists for their analyses, and the ethnographic reality of specific primitive cultures.

Another of his important contributions to economic anthropology was his analysis of value and exchange. He illustrated various categories of theoretical interest, and distinguished between the technological category of objects made for practical purposes, the ceremonial category of objects used as ritual tools and the economic category of objects which had an exchange value.

By distinguishing between the various forms of gift and exchange in the social and economic context of the Trobriand Islands, he highlighted significant criteria of general importance (Malinowski, 1922:182-195), such as "the regularity of transfer, the degree of customary sanction, immediacy of return, equivalence of return and the extent of bargaining". Furthermore, he openly introduced into the anthropological literature the concept of reciprocity, which was an invaluable tool in the study of the nature of transactions, if only because it helped focus attention on the possible implications of any simple transaction of goods or services, and located the transaction in its corresponding place within the overall system of transactions. In addition, he demonstrated that the "constant give and take, which governed tribal life" (Malinowski, 1922:173) tended to provide coherence and meaning to social life. As Goodfellow has indicated, Malinowski showed quite forcefully that a group or society did not remain united through some mystical impulse towards unity, but rather, in part, through "a deep-rooted tendency to create social ties through the exchange of gifts". Furthermore, the entirety of Malinowski's analysis indicated how this exchange of gifts symbolised and maintained social status (quoted by Firth, 1974 b:238).

Various criticisms can be made of Malinowski's treatment. According to the author cited above, his theoretical conception of economic value was unclear and he was eager to dispel the impression that economic values on the Trobriand Islands were simply a question of rational calculation. However, despite the vagueness of his assertions, he demonstrated his thesis that the components of economic value in primitive economic systems possessed a social content which could not be postulated *a priori*, but rather required an empirical examination of the complex social content, including an account of power and status, together with other factors of a more immediately practical nature. Thus, the value of food on the Trobriand Islands depended principally on its exhibition and ceremonial preparation, on its 'cultural qualities', on the enhancement of prestige through its possession, on the use to which surplus was put, ostentatiously left to rot, all of which formed part of a socialised 'sentiment' indirectly related to the pleasure of eating it: "This value renders accumulated food a symbol and vehicle of power" (Malinowski, 1922:177). However, although he examined this aspect in detail, he did not relate it to the problem of supply or how the value of food was determined, etc.

The market for *kula* valuables was also extremely elastic. However, Malinowski did not explore any processes of calculation for comparing the profitability of work invested in the production of food with work of another kind which might produce *kula* valuables. Similarly, he held that the value of manufactured objects depended on the satisfaction they gave as a result of the selection of the materials used, the perfection of their manufacture or the craftsman who produced them. But he did not discuss the repercussions that the investment of time and energy in producing these objects might have had on their value, above all bearing in mind that *kula* objects had no practical use in any sense of the word, and that the most elaborate pieces were too good to be used, rendering their possession all the more desirable.

Likewise, another great defect of Malinowski's analysis of exchange was the lack of any precise indication of how the value of *kula* objects was established. For objects of the same type, shell armbands on the one hand, and shell necklaces on the other, it is clear that considerations such as size, colour, and the history of previous exchanges must have been important. But in the *kula ring*, these objects were circulated in opposite directions, thus an object from one category was inevitably paired with an object from the other. As Firth asked (1974 b:241), what criteria were applied to do this? Malinowski did not give the quantitative data, particularly desireable where such variation in the individual objects existed, which would have enabled us to identify the relationship between objects of the same category. Perhaps it should be noted here that in *kula* transactions, the idea of equivalence was very strong and precise, so that we could expect a more systematic analysis of this concept, particularly since he did provide data on the exchange relationship. Marcel Mauss also complained that Malinowski did not explain the sanctions underlying *kula* reciprocity satisfactorily: "Was it a mystical and moral sanction?" he asked (1954:24).

Other criticisms have been made regarding the 'meaning' of the *kula*. It is true that Malinowski's chapter with this heading is weak, from a sociological point of view, leading Evans Pritchard (1951:95),to claim that Malinowski did not clearly delineate "what is perhaps the most important feature of the *kula*:the coming together of autonomous political communities through the acceptance of common ritual values". In a formal sense, he was right, but Malinowski (1921) had already indicated that the *kula* expeditions "connected the different island groups" and that they "represented a kind of inter-tribal relationship of unprecedented magnitude". Later, he again referred to the different districts engaged in the *kula* as different political units and asserted that a solid understanding of the main political institutions was essential in order to understand the *kula* (1922:79 and ss.). Likewise, he also stated that it was the symmetry and reciprocity of inter-tribal relationships and the individualism, as regards individual transactions and the permanence of partnership relationships, that gave the *kula* such significance.

The way in which a series of authors, such as Mauss and Labouret, Lenoir and Warnotte, have attempted to address the *kula* from a wider perspective is a good indication of the stimulus which Malinowski's work represented. This has been pointd out by Firth (1974 b:244 y ss.), citing Warnotte (1927:72), for example, who suggested that the *kula*, like *potlatch*, depended on certain economic, political and demographic characteristics:small groups operating over relatively extensive territories, relative social equality, or at least an unstable system of social subordination, and freedom from military domination. On the other hand, social control within these groups was relatively easy since each of the participants was personally known to the others. This highlights the fact that a system such as the *kula*, with its long-term credit, essentially depended on personal knowledge of each of the participants by the others. Warnotte also corroborated Malinowski's opinion that an important function of the *kula* might be that of providing symbols which helped to maintain Trobriand chiefdom in a part of Melanesia where social stratification was weak, and the tradition of chiefdom precarious.

Malinowski (1922:357 and ss.) also emphasised the growing importance of the *kula*, since it offered an opportunity for parallel commercial trade. Labouret (1953:24) accepted this view, further corroborated by Fortune (1932:208), and added the interesting point that the *kula* endowed overseas participants with a commercial monopoly which explained in part the importance it held. It is also clear from Malinowski's material, as Lenoir has demonstrated (1924:387, 394, 403), that a great deal of latent hostility was ritualised in the *kula*, and that there was a similarity in the relief of existing tension provided by the act of exchange and a peace treaty. However, from a sociological point of view, the *kula* would seem above all to offer, through the use and exchange of symbolic objects, a means of expressing, maintaining and establishing status on a scale impossible for any isolated Massim community.

In his published material, Malinowski paid scant attention to themes such as scarcity, social regulation of saving as regards food reserves, or the impact of the western economy on the Trobriand tribal economy. However, he mentioned pearl hunting and its relationship to the *kula* and the exportation of surplus crops to feed labourers employed by European colonials, and also conducted a brief comparison of the earnings obtained by natives employed by Europeans and those obtained by farmers. In addition, he referred to the decline in customs under European influence, but did not analyse the total effect on tribal economy of the possibility of producing a surplus for exportation, or the way in which availability of labour was affected before 1920.

According to Firth (1974 b:247) however, any criticism that can be made of the economic analysis presented by Malinowski is more than balanced by his positive contributions:for elucidating the system of credit; for his detailed description of socialised means of distribution, represented by the 'urigubu' gift of yams; for his meticulous dissection of the system of rights involved in land ownership; and for demonstrating the close relationship between political authority and economic control. He did not limit himself to analysing the Trobriand economy, but also showed how

Oscar Fernández

the system of economic mechanisms tended to maintain the structure of this society.

Whilst it is true that the body of his economic theory did not contribute greatly to specifically economic studies, nevertheless his contribution in marginal areas of economics was great. His conceptual universe was different to the formal and arid propositions of the times, and he preferred postulates about economic operations, which for him represented the richness of interpretation of real human conduct. In this way, Malinowski provided an immense stimulus to parallel analyses in other primitive economic systems with a low technological level, and posed some of the basic problems:problems of organisation of economic efforts; of material incentives compared to the social incentives of status and prestige; of the relationship between political and ritual leadership and the initiative and management of economic matters; of the economic implications of the use of social symbols; of the subtle composition of property rights; of the complexity of primitive market operations; and of the character of collective action in its social context.

The final aspect of *Argonauts* which cannot be overlooked refers to Malinowski's epistemological reflections, not only regarding field work and its problems, but also in terms of the goal which ethnographers should establish during the phase of interpreting the documents compiled and attempting to provide a meaning to the institutions studied. An example would be when he referred to the complexity of the *kula* and indicated that the actors were not consciously aware of the true purpose of the institution and were also unaware of the correlations existing between their own social structures. It was the duty of ethnographers, Malinowski said (1922:141-142), to uncover these questions, basing their accounts on the observation of concrete determining facts, and the final stage of their sociological work should be to construct an account which rendered intelligible the institution and its connections with the various elements of reality observed.

Argonauts is a 'truly functionalist' work, a functionalism in action in its manner of apprehending and subsequently explaining the elements of a complex reality, and in no way, according to Panoff (1974:37), a "dogmatic functionalism". Taken thus, the qualities offered by the book are evident:unity, coherence and a progressive development which maintains the reader's interest through providing the illusion of conducting the research personally. To Malinowski's interest for 'primitive beings' should be added a discovery generally ignored by ethnographers, namely, his clear awareness of the role played by aesthetic values in 'uncivilised' human life. These concepts constituted a novelty when *Argonauts of the Western Pacific* was published, and continue to be so today.

3.2. The Psychology of Kinship

Following publication of the *Argonauts*, Malinowski studied various questions of a psychological nature and published a series of articles, the most important of which include **The Father in Primitive Psycology** (Malinowski, 1927 b) and **Myth in Primitive Psychology** (1925) which would later form the first two sections of his book **Sex and Repression in Savage Society** (1927 a). It was at this point that he defined his position with respect to psychoanalysis, and more specifically, with respect to Freud's *Totem and Taboo*.

In its Spanish translation, the book *Sex and Repression in Savage Society* (1927 a) consists of two very different and disparate sections. In the first section of the book, parts I and II, Malinowski presented and discussed the research material he had compiled on the Trobriand Islands in the light of Freudian theory. In fact, what he did was simply to adapt Freudian terminology. In the second, more ambitious section, parts III and IV, he addressed Freud's theory directly, examining it from a more general point of view based on an established contrast between animality and humanity, and using this articulation to subsequently address the problem arising from the relationship between sociology and psychoanalysis.

The ethnographic data on sexuality and family life compiled on the Trobriand Islands revolved around the question that Malinowski posed, of whether a Freudian interpretation was applicable or not to the case of primitive societies. His aim was to analyse the factors judged decisive by Freud, examine whether they held true and explore the effects produced in the context of native society on the Trobriand Islands. This was a highly valuable experimental society, since descent was matrilineal, social stratification completely different from the class divisions in European society, and the indigeneous culture in question was diametrically opposed to the world of capitalism. In contrast to the patrilineal European family, where the man was at once husband, father and provider, the man in a Trobriand family was not considered to be the progenitor of the children born to his wife, due to the absolute ignorance of the natives regarding the physiology of conception, and consequently, the man had no rights over his offspring. For these latter, the powerful man who they respected and who was responsible for their material well-being was the mother's brother. Given that the wife was more independent of her husband, and also due to the power of attraction of the mother's brother, the nuclear family had a different balance and did not constitute the autonomous unit represented by a European family. What Malinowski found was that the oedipal complex did not constitute a universal phenomenon. However, far from presenting this as a refutation of Freud's thesis, he viewed it as the best proof of its validity, arguing that the oedipal crisis was an inevitable experience for the middle class European man and thus could not exist in the same form for a Trobriand native. To simplify, he claimed that a comparison of the two societies revealed on the one hand, a repressed desire to kill the father and marry the mother, and on the other, the temptation to wed the sister and kill the maternal uncle (1927 a:81-82). In other words, and as stated by Panoff (1974:58), Malinowski saw himself, no less, as continuing the work of Freud, with the merit of having given, through the systematic exploration of correlations between biological and sociological factors, a generalised form of the initial model of the oedipus complex.

Another question which Malinowski attempted to answer was how Melanesian culture differed from that other, complex society in which the Oedipus complex had been duly confirmed. However, in this respect, Malinowski only skimmed the surface:why become entangled in intricate symbolic interpretations when it is sufficient to let the facts speak for themselves? (1927 a:116). He abruptly decided to proclaim the primacy of the manifest content of dreams over their latent content, and his disagreement and rupture with psychoanalysis appears in parts III and IV of the book. Malinowski assigned himself the exclusive task of refuting the argument of *Totem and Taboo*, that is, the thesis that the Oedipus complex was the key to explaining how and why culture originated, and more specifically, Freud's aspiration to resolve historical and sociological problems on the basis of psychological discoveries whose formulation was random and could not be proven (Panoff, 1974:60).

From this point onwards, the failure of Malinowski's approach is widely recognised. He failed to examine the relationship between culture and instincts and he failed in his attempt to critique Freudian theory of infantile sexuality.

He did not accept the presence of a libido in children and invoked a strictly utilitarian concept of instinct; for Malinowski, only the biological purpose of behaviour (in this case, sexual behaviour) was of importance. To summarise, Malinowski refused to hear the word 'sexuality' if it was not in the conventional sense of an activity limited to the genital sphere, which does not appear until puberty. Consequently, he utterly rejected the very basis of Freudian theory, a posture which represented one of his advances which in later years would be confirmed more conclusively by other studies.

Nevertheless, Malinowski's debt to psychoanalysis is evident throughout much of his work, although nowhere as much as in his descriptions of the structure of Trobriand families and in the theory of kinship which he developed as a result. In fact, Fortes (1974:175) maintained that the concept of the Oedipus complex gave Malinowski the inspiration for the main features of his kinship theory. His accurate transposition of this concept to a 'matriarchal' context gave coherence and meaning to the apparently contradictory facts of Trobriand family relationships: "In this he found a mechanism capable of clearly explaining the coexistence, in a system of mutually opposed forces, of the different elements of the matrilineal family. Paternal love and the authority of the uncle, the sexual bond between spouses and the sexual barriers between siblings, the obligatory friendship and the common interests of the uncle and nephew together with the mutual enmity, the ignorance of physiological paternity, the incest taboo and the impulse to violate it, all had their place in a unified schema consistently constructed on the basis of a revised Freudian hypothesis."

It is in the works cited, *Sex and Repression* and *The Father* (Malinowski, 1927 a and b, respectively) where his greatest contributions to the theory of kinship appeared, namely his outline of the now classic system of matrilineal paternity divided between the father, united to the child by personal bonds of affection and care based on his exclusive sexual access to the mother and on his part in the task of rearing the child, and the mother's brother, linked to his sister's child by ties of rights and duties rooted in the prohibition of incest and in legal authority, accompanied by a repressed hostility. To summarise, he grouped all the above under the concept of a 'matrilineal complex' and, without doubt, adopted this point of view because he was more interested in the nuclear or conjugal family than in larger units (lineage, clan, etc.) since it was within this basic group that the rival influences on the individual exercised by the father's kin and the mother's kin were most clearly visible.

In Malinowski's conceptual schema, the facts of social relationships, organisation and groupings were simply aspects of custom and motivation, comparable in general terms to magical beliefs, for example, and ultimately generated by universal human instincts such as the parental instinct, or by common human sentiments such as vanity or ambition. Thus, nowhere in Malinowski's work is there an integrated analysis of local organisation, kinship and Trobriand political structure as an analytically discernible outline of social life. In other words, Malinowski did not pay sufficient attention to the need to see kinship relationships as a system within the tissue of the total social structure. In the case of the Trobriand Islanders, among whom the rules of rank directly influenced kinship behaviour, this was particularly important. On the contrary, in his analyses of these data, Malinowski paid more attention to emotions and sentiments, and only secondarily examined questions of rights and duties. This was a consequence of the psychological perspective that he had adopted, and was entirely congruent with the permanent struggle he identified between 'real' emotions and sentiments and 'ideal' laws and morals.

Rivers deserves to be mentioned here, for the influence he exerted, according to Fortes (1974:164), on Malinowski:firstly as the founder of field studies of primitive kinship; secondly, because he was considered an authority on the subject of Melanesian social organisation, and lastly, for what appeared to be his sociological theory of kinship, although he was unable to consider kinship as a sociological question. In his search for the 'social conditions' which in his opinion determined kinship systems, namely, the terminology of the relationship systems, what he actually described were the rules of matrimony, which he speculatively suggested had existed in the past. Rivers and what he represented explains to a great extent Malinowski's insistence on the 'biographical method', and especially his disdain for the "ridiculous algebra of kinship", which he developed in detail in an article specifically addressing this subject (Malinowski, 1930). Malinowski cited kinship terminology as an example of what he called "linguistic accumulation". His pragmatic theory of language, with its exaggeration of the instrumental meaning of words, as we will see later on, and his model of language acquisition as a conditioning process stemmed, in part, from his reaction to the dominant obsession for kinship terminology.

In the penultimate chapter of *Sex and Repression*, Malinowski looked at the comparative characteristics of descent systems. Basing his argument on the analyses conducted by Rivers and Lowie, Malinowski (1927 a:263-273) can be credited with clarifying what Panoff (1974:65-66) considered "a poorly posed problem", namely, the relationship between rules of descent (a principle sanctioned by laws or customs which automatically determined the genealogical connections through which, at birth, individuals would receive various elements particular to their condition) and the practical channels for accessing authority functions and which govern the distribution of a deceased person's goods. The distinction that Malinowski stressed between these three concepts was eminently useful at a time when it was common to speak of 'matriarchy' and 'patriarchy', dichotomous categories which served as global characterisations of an entire society. Nevertheless, Malinowski insisted on the dialectical nature of the relationships existing between these three elements and on the impossibility for society of ignoring those genealogical bonds which were not sanctioned by the rules of descent (bonds with the paternal line in a matrilineal society, for example).

Fortes (1974:196) has suggested that Malinowski's conceptual schema was not the most appropriate for the study of kinship systems as part of the total social structure. In a similar vein, Raymond Firth, who in his book *We, the tikopia* interpreted his field data according to Malinowski's proposed method, asserted that "what an anthropologist must study is kinship behaviour, and not kinship sentiments" (Firth, 1936:576), thus directly rejecting a psychological approach (as an aside, he also rejected the interpretation of social institutions in terms of basic human needs, but I will return to this later). However, in his defence it can be said that today it is considered essential for kinship studies to be based on observation of people's behaviour, their thoughts and their sentiments, more than on simple interrogation of a few chosen informants,

But where we can best appreciate the extent to which modern social science has adopted some of Malinowski's hypotheses is in the postulate that the nuclear family is the origin and principle cause of all kinship customs and behaviours. "The point of departure for an analysis of kinship is the nuclear family", stated Murdock (1949:92), citing Malinowski in support of his claim.

Fortes (1974:197 and ss.) established a somewhat curious relationship between Lévi-Strauss and Malinowski. On the one hand, Mauss's essay *The Gift*, which inspired Lévi-Strauss, was based in turn on Malinowski's analysis of exchange among the Trobriand Islanders:thus it would not be unreasonable to suggest that Lévi-Strauss was indirectly inspired by Malinowski. On the other, Fortes found a similarity between Malinowski's *Sex and Repression* (1927 a) and the study of marriage between cross cousins by Lévi—Strauss (1949), in the form, in some content and in the general conclusion:the prohibition of incest marks the transition from Nature to Culture.

In 1929, Malinowski published another important monograph, ***The Sexual Life of Savages of North-Western Melanesia***, which rapidly became a classic. As Havelock Ellis indicated in his preface to the book, its impact was due in part to the groundbreaking nature and sheer number of the facts presented, which indisputably constituted an authentic novelty for the times. Theoretical commentary is scarce, and was mainly provided in the prologue that Malinowski wrote three years later for the third edition, published in 1932. Here, he continued to develop the functional method and his 'theory of needs' (Malinowski, 1929:37-38), and also rewrote his definition of 'culture' written for the *American Encyclopoedia of the Social Sciencies* (Malinowski, 1931). It is not easy to summarise the most interesting feature of the book, bearing in mind its descriptive nature and the fact that it represented a reworking of other, already published texts, thus containing aspects which had already been addressed elsewhere in his work such as the sexual freedom of adolescents, native beliefs regarding procreation and the reincarnation of spirits or some aspects of kinship, although in this case, references to psychoanalysis were downplayed. Other themes corresponded to clarifications or rectifications of other works. For example, in *Argonauts* he had described the husband's obligation to provide his wife with "remuneration for the sexual services provided", a discovery which Marcel Mauss considered to be of great significance for the sociology of matrimony and economic anthropology, and he returned to this subject in *The Sexual Life* (1929:230-232). As regards the question of incest among the inhabitants of the Trobriand Islands, he maintained his stance in relation to an old controversy, pointing out the difference between the rules and actual practices (1929:357-360) in an attempt to underline the advantages of functionalism and its research methods when addressing this kind of question (Panoff, 1974:70).

However, as Havelock Ellis (Malinowski, 1929:52) suggested, it was highly possible that in describing sexual customs so very different to our own, "Malinowski contributed significantly to changing our way of judging different civilisations".

3.3. More than a monograph:*Coral Gardens and Their Magic*

In 1935, Malinowski published ***Coral Gardens and Their Magic, A study of the Methods of Tilling the Soil and of Agricultural Rites in the Trobriand Islands,*** two weighty volumes addressing the subject of growing crops on the Trobriand Isalnds and the associated magical practices. The second volume comprises a linguistic study of texts and notes in the vernacular language on this subject, and gives the impression of being highly technical.

The book itself is more than a monograph in the accepted sense in the human sciences, and is generally recognised as such. More so even than *Argonauts*, the book displays the talent and stylistic quality of Malinowski's writing and confirms that, in this respect, a comparison with Joseph Conrad, to summarise Malinowski's own ambition, would merit serious consideration. Furthermore, there is a human quality to it which gives a tone that would be inconceivable in a conventional monograph, to such an extent that Panoff (1974:72) asserted that Malinowski, "despite his scientific protestations, is also an author who participates fully in what he describes and thus, he depicts for us the Trobriand Island natives in such a way that he sets them apart forever from any other 'savages' who might exist".

As in his previous works, in this book he once again revealed a constant concern for the totality. From the title, one might think that the book dealt only with crop growing techniques and associated rituals, but this is not the case, rather, this was the lens through which Trobriand civilisation was viewed. Taking horticulture as the point of departure, the various aspects of Trobriand culture were rendered intelligible. The exchange of food, the ostentatious practices associated with crops, solidarity between kin, the function of the chief in economic regulation and even the shape of the architectural structures used to store yams were all given form and meaning in the narrative. The care taken of the gardens and their aesthetic refinement, and even the native concept of a garden as a *work of art*, were not considered less relevant than other discoveries in the book, such as the role of magic and the magician who appears throughout the description.

In all of Malinowski's work, and perhaps most clearly in this book in particular, his concerns moved on two levels: that of the specific society of the Trobriand Islanders, among whom he carried out his field work and thus understood to perfection, and that of humans and society in general. Although at times he used data from other, more or less similar societies, he never did so in strictly comparative terms. In his theoretical writings, his generalisations leapt directly from the Trobriand Islanders to humanity in general, and it seems indisputable that he saw Trobriand society as particularly instructive. This propensity to generalise is most clearly visible in his treatment of subjects such as magic and religion, where it is also evident that he strived to prove that such a propensity was legitimate.

The fundamental dogma of his theory concerning magic was that this was a manifestation of the inevitable human effort to achieve satisfaction, however illusory, of violent and unattainable desires. According to Nadel (1974:205), Malinowski located primitive man in a world in which his technical skills and his capacity for rational thought merely provided him with confidence in himself and a limited control of environmental conditions. Within these limits, he could confidently apply the knowledge he had acquired through ordinary experience. Beyond them, his knowledge was of no use. It is here that magic came into play "as a complement to the skills acquired and rational knowledge" (Malinowski, 1944:173), as an extension of human effort beyond its natural sphere:as something above and beyond the tools and strength of man which helped control chance and trick fate (Malinowski, 1931:109). In other words, as a power which extended beyond the normal world.

This 'beyond' has several meanings. One of these refers to the aspect of luck in life. Malinowski frequently cited an example from the Trobriand Islands which corroborated this argument: "fishing along the coastline, being safe and easy, does not require magic. In contrast, navigation and deep sea fishing mobilise all the paraphernalia of a fully developed fishing magic" (*Ibíd.*:112).

A second meaning of the expression 'beyond the normal' refers to the domain of truly miraculous achievements, impossible to attain through 'normal' means. The myths described an age of miracles of this type when canoes could fly and old men were capable of rejuvenation. However, these were not necessarily spectacular events "since normal human beings were involved". Any repeated magical ritual in which there is belief, any event "in which supernatural forces intervene as cause or effect" is one of these miracles. "It is only through magic that an ugly man who women would normally reject, can hope to become attractive" (Malinowski, 1922:302).

Thirdly and lastly, the effects of magic may go 'beyond' the normal in a double sense, material and moral. This is the domain of balck magic, sorcery and witchcraft, the domain of evil miracles. To kill is evil:at a distance, a miracle. Nadel (1974:207) stated that it is in explaining this evil magic where Malinowski's interpretation is weakest: "If the essence of magic is its promise to provide (primitive) man with control of the risks and dangers associated with his surrounding world, why has this primitive man had to add risk on risk, danger on danger by inventing black magic and malign witchcraft?" he asked. Malinowski gave two replies. One was that black magic originated in "the natural human reaction to frustrated hate and impotent rage", which was merely a variant, equally passionate, of love magic (Malinowski, 1931:111). The other, that belief in magic must protect itself against the weakness threatened by failure.

The need for a magic in which one can believe generates the belief in a magic one should fear. Behind all this lies a more general psychological principle: "such is human nature" that men's desires are not satisfied merely by being attained, but rather by impeding others from attaining theirs. And this is the ultimate source of belief in black magic (Malinowski, 1955:65-66).

Faced with the insecurity of certain situations, and faced with the "horror of meaningless inherent in human nature", the mentality of humans pushes them towards some kind of activity. Magic is an activity which allows humans to feel that they are 'in harmony with life': "magic ritualises optimism" (Malinowski, 1955:61 and 70).

However, as we have seen, the way in which Malinowski treated magic opened new perspectives, and his pragmatic interpretation applied to primitive economies revealed the economic role of magic. Thus, in *Coral Gardens* he amply demonstrated how magic served to organise work and control cooperative efforts. But he also believed that the heart of the magical process was the formula or spell, enunciated exactly and without variation, and thus he explored all the linguistic parallels of magic in the second volume of the book, insisting better than anyone on the importance of language in the study of these practices. The procedures he employed were another question.

Malinowski (1922:422) argued that the native was convinced of the mysterious and intrinsic power of forms of language, of the magic inherent in words that could bring any desired object within reach and of the effectiveness of the accompanying gestures. However, Nadel (1974:211) stated that such a subjective interpretation did not explain why the *corpus* of general knowledge on magic exerted such an objective attraction, even on the most dispassionate of people. Here arose the controversy over whether magic represented the primitive equivalent of science or not. Malinowski's stance on this issue was clear. In his opinion, magic and science were similar in that they both proposed specific goals, used specific techniques and were of a strictly practical nature. However, although magic could be called a 'pseudoscience', it could not be likened to science. Even at the most primitive level, magic and science coexisted alongside one another as two elements of a different substance in form and function, each of them "controlling different aspects of human behaviour" (Malinowski, 1944:197) and "mobilising diverse social contexts and traditions, one profane and the other sacred, surrounded by observances, mysteries and taboos" (Malinowski, 1955:67). In addition to being dominated by emotion, magic was "indisputably supernatural and occult". Whereas magic promised primitive man miracles, science defined the limit of his rational efforts and of his skills based on experience.

He also attempted to introduce a precise distinction with regard to the problem of the limits of magic and religion. Magic and religion were similar in that both arose from and emotional tension similar to that experienced in life crises, such as the recognition that the control humans can exercise over the universe using reason and empirical skills is tragically limitied. They were similar in that both had their own mythology, miracles, taboos and observances, which separated the sacred from the profane (Malinowski, 1955:87). However, although both represented advoidance of the issue of human impotance, they differed radically in the nature of evasion they represented. Magic was characterised by the limitations of its techniques and its practical orientation, whereas religion constituted a set of acts which represented an end in themselves, with a complex content expressed in rituals and beliefs which had 'value' but not practical purpose. Magic was based on a simple belief in the effectiveness of spells and rituals, whilst religion governed "the entire supernatural world of faith", with a pantheon of gods, spirits and benevolent powers. Whereas the mythology of magic was limited to "boasting about primaeval successes", religious mythology was converted into a cosmogony, and opened the perspective of an afterlife. Magic was in the hands of specialists, or experts, whilst religion was "everybody's business", and the specialisation of priests or visionaries "does not represent a profession but rather a personal gift". Lastly, whereas magic could be good, but also bad, and was concerned with 'doing things' (positive magic) or undoing the attainments of others (negative magic), religion was essentially moral and addressed irreversible events (Malinowski, 1955:88-90.).

From this comparison, Nadel (1974:215) concluded that Malinowski was incapable of seeing religion without an undertone of magic. Some other passages even suggest that for Malinowski, religion was little more than a bigger and better type of magic. But this point by point comparison shows that the problem of the limits which separated them was a real and important one. In religion and magic, he saw two opposing but complementary forms of transcendental belief. Magic and religion were opposed because magical acts were not only utilitarian but also instrumental, with a widely recognised purpose in that they were simply a means to achieve a concrete end (Malinowski, 1955:20; 1935, I:455). Religious acts lacked purpose in this sense, or the ritual and the purpose were one and the same thing, and the end was achieved through the very consummation of the act (Malinowski, 1955:21, 23).

Another aspect which Malinowski highlighted was the socialisation of death which resulted from the paradigmatic importance of the psychology of religion. Furthermore, for Malinowski, the rituals surrounding death were more than a paradigm:they indicated the true source from which religion must have sprung. Death, he claimed, was the ultimate crisis in the lives of individuals and the community, the event which caused most distress and disorder. The sentiments of terror and horror were not predominant in the attitude of primitive peoples to death, but rather appeared mixed with love for the dead, for those whom they had personally loved. This ambivalent attitude was manifest in the manner of disposing of the dead, the desire to conserve them and advoid the transformation produced by death, and the desire to maintain ties with the deceased but at the same time, to break those ties.Within the context of this psychological crisis, a new idea was born of a future life and the survival of the spirit. Although all this appears to refer primarily to the emotional conflicts of the individual and to the role of religion as a solution and consolation, social factors also intervened. Humans, who live "in cooperation and mutual assistance all their lives" cannot easily bear the dissolution of these bonds when life ceases. Consequently, belief in human immortality, the basis for ancestor worship, sprang from the very nature of human society (Malinowski, 1931:120). In the last resort therefore, it is the existence of society and involvement in social relationships which generated the veneration of death and the concept of immortality (Malinowski, 1955:47 and ss.). The personal crisis that death represents is at the same time a social crisis, given that the sentiments wounded by death are sentiments born of social relationships. According to Malinowski, two effects were combined:since religion stopped humans from giving free rein to their fear and horror, which would lead to the disintegration of the group and the culture, it reestablished solidarity and morale and ensured continuity of social existence. In addition, since religion offered humans the promise of immortality, it taught them to "act in concert with past and future generations" (Malinowski, 1931:130).

Malinowski asserted that any religious function, for example defending the moral values of the group, could only be achieved "through individual mental attitudes". In consequence, religion was not entirely social, but rather "to a large extent springs from purely individual sources" (1955:41). However, Malinowski did not arrive at a balanced posture and this was no doubt due to the ideas he had inherited in which an erroneous antithesis between individual and society still persisted, and where the 'individual mind' was maintained apart from any 'social' contamination (Nadel, 1974:218). Thus, he argued against the assumption that humans had an instinctive propensity for religion, and against the idea that religion was simply a cultural and social imposition. In fact, religion presented some of both aspects: it reflected a derived but deeply-rooted need. It was a need derived from the social organisation within which humans acted and lived, and through which they ensured their biological existence. Since it was this very social existence which gave rise to so much mental conflict, religion, by offering a means to resolve this conflict, contributed to human survival, or at least to the survival of humans in society.

If Malinowski's treatment of religion and magic opened new doors, his interpretation of myth was entirely revolutionary, to the extent that today we use some of his formulations as if they were self-evident. The clearest example of this, according to Nadel (1974:222), is his key expression *mythic charter*. His revolutionary idea was that he denied the explanatory and symbolic function of myth. Myth was an important narrative in establishing the existing social order and in justifying sacred precedents, its warranty or *mythic charter*. "The function of myth consists in strengthening tradition and endowing it with greater value and prestige by elevating it to the initial reality of events, more supernatural and more effective" (Malinowski, 1931:119). But there were other aspects of myth which could serve entirely different purposes. Myths could occupy the place of poetry or epic: "the mythology of the Trobriand *kula*, for example, also provides one of the basic elements of tribal life. Myth enriches the manner in which people perceive the world around them, filling the landscape with dramatic events and giving it meaning. Myth is a living thing which attempts to provide a total history of the world from its creation to what we know as the present, with its living customs and institutions, and which cannot clearly determine a limit in the time between this previous period and the present" (Malinowski, 1922:296-301).

At the end of volume I of *Coral Gardens* (1935:465-488, reproduced in part in Malinowski, 1975), Malinowski presented a self-criticism supported by a series of positive reflections which constituted a methodological approach of great use as regards the difficulties inherent in field work. He lamented his ignorance of botany, his incomplete compilation and his mistaken attempt to orientate the research towards land ownership (Malinowski, 1935, I:336-344). In contrast, Panoff (1974) accused him of having shown a lack of curiosity in the study of magic, and felt that this was the book's greatest failing, above all from the point of view of the problems of symbolism: "but Malinowski could not see these without disengaging himself from his own mental universe. He was so concerned with utilitarianism in his interpretation of cultural phenomena that he was unable to take what was said in magical incantations or the ritual gestures which accompanied their recitation, seriously. For him it was sufficient to have discovered the supervisory function exercised by the sorcerer as regards sentiment and emotion, and considered the subject closed. If Malinowski made an important discovery in understanding that the sorcerer acted as the 'boatswain' of economic activities among the Trobriand natives, at the same time he turned his back on a more diaphanous ethnographic reality, regarding magic as a simple phenomenon of affection which in itself would be pointless to study" (Panoff, 1974:74).

According to Nadel (1974:224), perhaps the best aspect of Malinowski's contribution to the study of religious beliefs was that he found a new way to consider these phenomena and a new logic within them, which his successors would continue to develop even though this logic was that of rationality. Magic, religion and mythology had to have meaning, "although this would often be simplified and resemble common sense too closely, his research constituted a good guide for his successors".

3.4. Malinowski and the language of magic

In the introduction to *Coral Gardens,* Malinowki (1935) revealed himself to be particularly proud of the second volume, *The Language of Magic and Gardening,* since it offered "a complete ethnographic contribution from the point of view of language".

One noteworthy aspect of this linguistic study was that Malinowski constituted an exception as regards British Social Anthropology, which had always shown scant interest in the subject. Perhaps encouraged by his links with J. R. Firth, the first professor of General Linguistics in England and the founder of the *London School of Linguistics*, or perhaps for other reasons, the fact is that he invested much of his energy in developing a 'linguistic theory of primitive languages'. Among the reasons that the British school of Socail Anthropology considered the study of language to be outside its scope, Henson (1974:38) indicated the fact that the science of language was already an autonomous, well-established discipline whereas anthropology was still trying to establish its interests and rules. Thus, instead of developing their own approach to language, anthropologists assumed that the subject was already adequately addressed by linguists, and in many cases, where linguistics entered into anthropological discussions, its use was based on the application of theories already established by Indoeuropean linguistics.

When Malinowski began his field work in Kiriwina, he conducted surveys and constructed genealogies using *Pidgin English*, although "the material thus compiled is never more than dead material" (Malinowski, 1922:23). Later, in the course of his field work, he realised the need to acquire knowledge of the native tongue, and it was in this language that he subsequently conducted his research. There is evidence of this in all his ethnographic writings, and more specifically, in a comment on his work with the Mailu (Malinowski, 1915:109): "I'm afraid that I must explicitly boast and be proud of my ability to acquire and converse in a foreign language". This ability may also have influenced the importance that he gave as an ethographer to language. Nevertheless, he also admitted his lack of linguistic preparation, above all during his first stay on the Trobriand Islands, on Kiriwina, from 1915 to 1916, a problem which he attempted to remedy for his subsequent visit. During the period that he was writing *Coral Gardens and Their Magic*, he claimed to have read more on linguistics than on any other aspect of anthropology (Malinowski, 1935:II, xi), in order to construct his so-called 'Ethnographic Theory of Language'.

This theory, if he can be said to have constructed it, appears not only in *Coral Gardens* but also in three other works, namely, *Classificatory Particles in the Language of Kiriwina* (1920), *The Argonauts* (1922) and in *The Problem of Meaning in Primitive Languages* (1923). In *Coral Gardens* (1935), he would once again return to what he had already discussed in these previous works.

In the first article, **Classificatory Particles in the Language of Kiriwina**, Malinowski (1920) called the Kiriwina language a 'native language' rather than a savage or primitive one, because these would be 'crude and mistaken words'. In doing so, he located the language alongside any other language spoken in any part of the world, but differentiated it from what are known as 'modern languages'. He added that "much, apparently excellent work has recently been conducted on the native languages of America" which he was ignorant of. But he was not a linguist and the sources he used were the same as those which had been used by generations of anthropologists before him. What he tried to do was to record, describe and explain the classificatory particles which he said appeared in combination with all numbers, possessives and adjectives. These varied according to the noun they modified. He gave what he called a "complete list of particles and the noun types with which each is associated". However, this apparently systematic approach was not followed by an exhaustive treatment of the particles, which he grouped according to their meaning without attempting to give a structural definition of them. Rather, he tried to show how they functioned, translating them into an English lacking in meaning. One significant aspect of his explanation was his recourse to his ethnographic material in order to explain meaning. For example, he said that no particle was associated with the activity of counting yams because, he claimed, given their importance, "counting yams is to count *par excellence'* (Malinowski, 1920:53).

Although he offered many specific details, he used them to establish certain generalisations. He started with a formulation within his functionalism: "all aspects of tribal life are related. Trying to separate them would result in mutilating all of them, and language is no exception in this respect" (*Ibíd.*:33). He argued that the most positive aspect of the study of a language was the light it shed on the social psychology of its speakers. Accordingly, Malinowski believed, in principle, that language was the reflection of thought. However, he was not entirely certain about this affirmation (and in fact, would later assert the contrary): "the nature of the correlation between the structure of a language and social psychology, the manner in which a language sheds light on the native mentality, would seem to be only partially comprehensible".

Faced with the difficulties posed by traditional grammatical particles (noun, verb, adjective) for the kind of language he was trying to describe, he opted for the solution of a linguistic theory based on meaning: "only from semantics . . . can the ethnographer obtain help" (*Ibíd.*:35). In conclusion, he stressed that the development of his own argument depended on meaning. But 'meaning' in the context of native languages always requires a reference to ethnographic descriptions, and thus, "linguistics without ethnography would fare as badly as ethnography would without the light thrown on it by language" (*Ibíd.*:78). In a brief and tentative reference, Malinowski asserted that "I can say at last that I have a semantic theory of my own, and that it was only thus that I felt capable of giving a certain consistency to my grammatical conclusions" (*Ibíd.*:74). However, it is difficult to see how this helped in reaching any grammatical conclusion. He emphasised the importance of contextualising the problem of meaning, and offered it as the only solution to what he considered "a completely new linguistic problem".

To summarise, in this work he identified the need for a ethnolinguistic theory which he himself attempted to provide: "A theory which serves as a guide to linguistic research conducted among natives in connection with ethnographic studies. A theory which does not serve for hypothetical reconstructions of origins, historical development or cultural transfer, nor for other similar speculations, but which is concerned with the intrinsic relationships between the facts. A theory which shows us what is essential in a language:how linguistic forms are influenced by physiological, mental and social factors, and other, cultural factors; the true nature of meaning and form, and the connection between them; a theory, in conclusion, which gives us a set of plastic, well-grounded definitions of grammatical concepts" (*Ibid.:*69).

Although *Argonauts of the Western Pacific* dealt principally with the *kula*, Malinowski also presented a further series of ethnographic data concerning the language, above all in the chapter entitled "The power of words in magic:some linguistic data", and in a series of references spread throughout the book. In the introduction, Malinowski (1922:22-23) emphasised the importance of maintaining records in the native language. He saw use of the native language as the tool which marked a great divide between his own field work and that which had been carried out by previous generations. He spoke of his facility for languages and of his increasingly abundant field notes written in Kiriwina, to which he referred as his *Corpus Inscriptionum Kiriwinienseium*, and which he said would be published separately later and would constitute the second volume of *Coral Gardens* (1935).

Malinowski found magic especially problematic and, according to Henson (1974:48), it was almost certainly his large collection of written magical spells which drove him to pose the problem of meaning. Trobriand spells contained words and expressions which were not used in normal conversation, and on this basis Malinowski examined the problem of translation. "Given that it is impossible to make sense of the translation of the spells, the meaning of these must go beyond a simple word by word translation". Thus, Malinowski's hypothesis was that the meaning of a text is the same as what it does, in other words, its meaning was the same as its function. This is Malinowski's meaning in the 'widest sense'. As J. R. Firth (1974:112) remarked, this recalls British empiricism, radicalism and philosophical utilitarianism, developed under the influence of the Vienna Circle. As J. R. Firth commented, "Wittgenstein would agree with the Malinowski's opinions on meaning. He said:'the meaning of words is in their usage. One cannot conjecture how a word functions. It is necessary to look at how it is used and learn from that' (Wittgenstein, 1953:80 and 109)".

Since the meaning is comparable to the sense given when translated into our own language, the result is that Malinowski's comments on linguistic translation were often extremely ethnocentric, in so far as they were always an approximation to the meaning from outside, in other words, from the reader rather from the Trobriand Islander. Thus he wrote "it would be good to take a series of phrases and show that it is necessary to add many ideas from sociological and ethnographic knowledge in order to render them intelligible" (Malinowski, 1922:458).

Using his collection of texts in the native language, in *Argonauts* Malinowski constructed one of his basic dogmas of anthropology. He used them to demonstrate the mentality of the native, and explained them by integrating them into the rest of his ethnographic data. But once again he revealed his uncertainty over whether language is a reflection of thought or not.

The article ***The Problem of Meaning in Primitive Languages*** was published in 1923, one year after *Argonauts*, as a supplement to the book by Ogden and Richard *The Meaning of the Meaning* (Malinowski, 1923). Given that this was devoted specifically to meaning, Malinowski's ideas appear in greater detail and are more fully developed than in his previous writings. He insisted on the importance of linguistics for anthropology, and even classified it as the "most important section of the general science of culture". He stressed his interest in problems of translation: "when, working with linguistic material, I tried to translate my texts into English and at the same time write a vocabulary and grammar of the language, I encountered great difficulties" (Malinowski, 1923:316). Using a brief text on navigation, he attempted to demonstrate that word for word translation was insufficient to reach the true meaning for the English reader, showing how the native language was used in a different manner to our own. Thus he arrived at the point, in section III, where he introduced the concept of *situational context* "if I may be permitted to coin an expression which indicates on the one hand that the concept of context should be expanded, and on the other, that the situation in which the words are offered can never be described by something as immaterial as linguistic expression (*Ibid.*:324).

This was a key concept in his semantic theory of native languages which, according to J. R. Firth (1974:121-122), had its roots in Dr. Philipp Wegener's *situational theory*. This proposed that unless a language was studied in its situational context, mutual understanding and cooperation would not be achieved by the language alone. The situation was the baseline and context of all the facts and data, and the effective processes of speaking and listening happened within it. He distinguished three kinds of situation:firstly, the objective situation as presented and observed; secondly, the elements which memory associates with that situation, or the recall factor; and thirdly, the situation of the mental state in its entirety (with particular reference to self-awareness or the personal identity of all participants). All these completed the meaning of the content of each specific language. However, Malinowski, with his dependence on linguistic context, once again revealed his ethnocentricity through his rather naïve linguistic assessment of the language as a basically inadequate and limited entity.

In order to show how the language was used, Malinowski described a fishing expedition, depicting how the discourse used was an integral part of helping to coordinate the behaviour of participants, and how it was full of technical terminology the same as if it were a modern scientific text. From this he deduced that in primitive usage, language functioned as an element of coordinated human activities, as a part of human behaviour. It was a mode of action, and not an instrument of reflection. "Language, in its primitive function, is to be regarded as a mode of action rather than as a countersign for thought" (Malinowski, 1923:313). In other words, language according to Malinowski did not express thought. I feel it is unnecessary to list the criticisms he received on this point.

With the purpose of arguing this idea, Malinowski introduced a further series of concepts which were as vague and undefined as his *situational context*. Thus for example, he spoke of *phatic communication*: "a type of speech in which ties of union are created by a mere exchange of words". In these cases, the situation consisted of "what happens linguistically" (*Ibíd.*:334-335). Here, he invoked non-linguistic behaviour, but again, in the sense of language as action.

The article closes with a section on universal gramatical categories, in the most traditional and ineffective sense since it did not represent any particular difference from or advance on the ideas expressed in *Classificatory Particles*.

More than a decade later, in 1935, Malinowski published *Coral Gardens and Their Magic*. As mentioned previously, Malinowski was especially proud of the second volume, ***The Language of Magic and Gardering***, considering it a complete ethnographic contribution from the point of view of language. However, the vision he presented contained few changes from earlier contributions, and he even continued to use the grammatical categories of Indoeuropean languages. He insisted on the importance of language as the most powerful tool of ethnography, and returned to the problem of translation as an important part of his theory. In the chapter entitled "On translating untranslatable words", he even elevated the question to the status of a *fundamental anthropological problem.*

The method he described and used to translate a text was the same as that which he had already used in *Argonauts* and in other works. After situating the text from a sociological point of view, for example, a particular form of spell, he proceeded to his linguistic explanation of 'meaning'. First, he produced a word for word 'interlinear translation', a translation he also called "literal" or "verbatim", then he gave a free translation to 'everyday English'. Next, he collated both translations and this led him to a detailed commentary which he called "contextual specification of meaning", but with reference to the text, not the situation (J. R. Firth, 1974:126 and ss.). He introduced the term 'fixed meaning', that is, the fixed meaning that each native word had in English, and based on this, his theory of homonyms:strictly speaking, each time that a word was used in a different context, with slight variations, it should have a different meaning. Nevertheless, later he would in practice distinguish between 'accidental homonyms' and 'cognate homonyms' or similar.

To summarise, Malinowski's really successful and most productive idea about language was his recommendation that all field work be conducted in the context of the native language. The remainder of his contribution is widely considered by the majority of linguists to be unsatisfactory, especially as regards his treatment of the texts. Figure 4 below provides a synthesis of his theory of language.

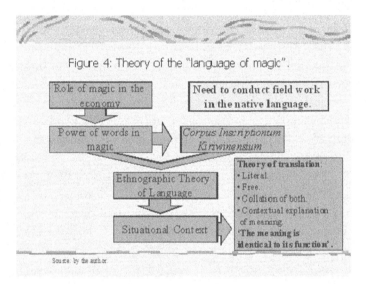

Figure 4: Theory of the "language of magic".

Source: by the author.

4. THE THEORY OF CULTURE AND OTHER CONSIDERATIONS.

A s we have seen, Malinowski's theory was inherent in all his work, although, as Lévi-Strauss said, in the most moderate opinion on Malinowski that he ever gave, he was a "better observer than he was a theoretician". But the effectiveness of his talent stemmed essentially from his inability to distance himself from form. This, which was fundamental in his writings, got lost from view in his later works published posthumously, a series of works which I will discuss in this section. These have been classified both as monotonous and boring, and as surprising and educational. Perhaps the most noteworthy of these is his *A Scientific Theory of Culture*, published in 1944, two years after his death, and which according to Panoff (1974:77) constitutes "a functionalist catechism written by a professor anxious to occupy his seat on the Academy, to captivate his students and eclipse his colleagues". First I will comment on this book, which brings together and systemises his theoretical contributions made throughout his work, and then I will turn to other writings which contain studies of cultural change or refer to the field work which he conducted in Mexico during his period in the United States.

4.1. The Theory of Needs

Within his encylopaedic definition of culture as "an integrated whole composed of consumer goods and tools, of the institutional charters of various social groups, of human ideas and skills, of beliefs and of customs, where, regardless of whether the society is primitive or developed, we will always find a vast material, human and spiritual apparatus through which man is capable of tackling the specific, concrete problems he faces" (Malinowski, 1944:36), and in the methodology he developed for studying culture, Malinowski introduced one of the most ambitious aspects of his theoretical approach, the 'Theory of Needs'. This theory appears throughout all his writings, but particularly in the article I have already discussed, *Culture*, published in 1931 in his posthumous book ***A scientific theory of culture*** (Malinowski, 1944).

The point of departure that Malinowski proposed (1931:96) was that humans, like any other animal, need to eat and reproduce in order to continue existing as individuals and as a species. They also need protection from the dangers posed by the physical environment, animals and other humans. They need to meet a wide range of bodily needs, including the need for shelter, heat, somewhere dry to sleep and a means to keep clean. Satisfying these primary bodily needs involves each culture in certain fundamental aspects such as institutions for food and supplies and for finding a partner and reproduction, and organisations for defence and comfort. These *organic* needs of humans constitute the basic imperatives that have led to the development of culture, in that they have obliged each community to implement a certain number of organised activities. Religion and magic, upholding the law or systems of knowledge and of mythology arise with such a constant regularity in all cultures that it can be concluded that they are also the result of our deepest needs or imperatives.

By need, Malinowski understood "the system of conditions which, in the human organism, in the cultural context and in the relationship of both with the natural environment, are inevitable and sufficient for the survival of the group and the organism. A need is, therefore, a limiting series of facts. Habits and their motivations, learnt responses and the basics of organisation must all be adapted in such a way as to enable basic needs to be met" (Malinowski, 1944:90). Beginning with the "system of conditions in the human organism", Malinowski asserted that determined biological impulses were met through a series of 'vital sequences'. These he enumerated as shown in Table 1.

This Table refers to the satisfaction of individual impulses. It highlights the dynamic bases of 'human nature' envisaged as an individual organism. According to Piddington (1974:41 n.3), Malinowski felt that it was extremely important that "the scholar should never forget that at the centre of all these institutions is a flesh and blood, living and breathing, human being". However, this list of impulses only corresponds indirectly to what he called the **basic needs** of humans as an animal species, because at this level individual and group survival needs must be added to individual impulses.

Table 1: Vital sequences incorporated in all cultures

Impulse	Act	Satisfaction
Urge to breathe	Inhalation of oxygen	Elimination of CO_2
Hunger	Eating food	Sensation of fullness
Thirst	Drinking liquids	Hydration
Sexual appetite	Copulation	Detumescence
Fatigue	Rest	Restored muscular and nervous energy
Restlessness	Activity	Satisfaction of fatigue
Somnolenscence	Sleep	Restored energy upon awakening
Bladder pressure	Miction	Disappearance of tension
Pressure on the colon	Defecation	Abdominal relaxation
Fear	Flight from danger	Relaxation
Pain	Avoidance using an effective method	Return to normal state

Source:Malinowski, 1984:98.

For this reason, Malinowski saw the need to add a Table of basic needs which reflected the totality of conditions necessary for individual and group survival, and not only individual impulses. The model he proposed is shown in Table 2.

Table 2: Basic needs and cultural responses.

Basic needs	Cultural responses
Metabolism	Provisioning
Reproduction	Kinship
Personal care	Shelter
Safety	Protection
Movement	Activity
Growth	Training
Health	Hygiene

Source:Malinowski, 1984:112.

Given that this schema could be applied to pre-human animals and primates, it would be the anatomical and physiological differences between animals and humans which indicated some of the fundamental and universal differences shown by human culture, such as technology, activities requiring forethought and collective planning and the various manifestations of symbolism, in particular those which referred to standards of behaviour and permitted the emergence of values. Anatomical and physiological developments, said Malinowski, not only facilitated the development of culture but also rendered it necessary.

Thus, culture held a value for biological survival. Its adaptability was in part due to the fact that although the basic needs that humans share with animals originated in primary determinism ["man does not live by bread alone, but first and foremost, he lives by bread" (Malinowski, 1944:72)], the conditions of life for humans as a social animal imposed a secondary determinism. In other words, he believed that the cultural means of satisfying human biological needs created "new conditions and in this way imposed new cultural imperatives" (Malinowski (1931:105), which he defined in terms of ***derived imperatives or needs***. Given that these were essentially a means to an end, they could also be termed *instrumental imperatives* of culture, and were closely related to the requirements for maintaining the cultural apparatus, regulation of human behaviour, socialisation and the exercise of authority. The responses to these *derived imperatives* or *needs* were embodied in the economy, social control, education and political organisation, as shown in Table 3.

Table 3. Cultural imperatives and the corresponding responses.

Imperatives	Responses
* The cultural apparatus of tools and consumer goods must be produced, used, amintained and replaced by new production.	Economy
* The technical, customary, legal or moral prescrriptions for human behaviour must be codified in actions and sanctions.	Social control

* The human material required to maintain all institutions must be renewed, trained, practised and provided with all knowledge pertaining to tribal tradition.	Education
* Authority within each institution must be defined, assigned power and provided with the means to compel compliance with orders.	Political organisation

Source:Malinowski, 1984:148.

However, even adding this list to the list of basic needs did not exhaust the imperatives imposed on humans. With slight verbal variations, it could be applied to sub-human organisms with a highly developed cortex. These are able to learn determined individual habits, but cannot transmit behavioural rules. To address this question of learnt behavioural habits essential to human life, Malinowski also incorporated what he called *integrative imperatives* by which "habit is transformed into custom; parental care into systematic education of the new generation, and impulses into values". The key to the entire process, according to Piddington (1974:44), resides in the symbolism that Malinowski argued would be found to be present in the birth of culture:the transition to human existence, namely culture, occurred when 'Eolithic' man first recognised the difference between good and bad—in technology, hunting techniques or in personal relationships—and began to inculcate these standards in the younger generation.

To the sphere of *integrative imperatives*, therefore, belonged those phenomena related to aspects such as tradition (including culturally recognised and transmitted social structures), standards and values, religion, art and ceremony, language and knowledge and other forms of symbolism, as shown in Table 4,

Table 4: Integrative imperatives.

INTEGRATIVE IMPERATIVES		
Tradition (social structure)		
Standards and values		
Religion, art and ceremony.		
Language and other forms of symbolism		
Habit	⟶	Custom
Parental care	⟶	Education
Impulses	⟶	Values

Source:by the author.

The satisfaction of basic human needs by traditional human institutions was a constant theme in Malinowski's work. Questions of social inheritance, popular in the 1930s, led him to develop his idea of secondary needs.

Figure 5 depicts a representation of his 'theory of needs' developed by the author. Here, it can be seen that when the group intervenes in resolving 'individual impulses', 'basic needs' are created. These are satisfied according to the different conditions of life and anatomical and physiological differences, giving rise to 'derived needs'. In turn, these, through the intervention of the symbolism of each culture, lead to the emergence of 'integrative imperatives'.

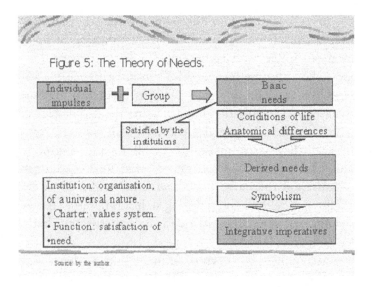

Figure 5: The Theory of Needs.

Source by the author.

If humans cannot satisfy biological processes such as nutrition, reproduction or defence without the help of rules, then culture must be considered an artificial or secondary environment absolutely essential to human survival. This reasoning was at the root of Malinowski's analysis of culture as a series of imperatives, or "conditions which must be met if the community is to survive", and of his conception of *institutions* as "the means to organise activities aimed at resolving these needs", and it also constituted an important part of his work.

The division into basic or instrumental, derived or integrative needs was not an especially fruitful one as the basis for collecting and analysing ethnographic data, nor for developing theory. The different imperatives overlapped too much and the division was difficult to apply. But the concept of institution which resulted from his study of needs did not suffer from these limitations and has demonstrated its usefulness in data collection and analysis.

In accordance with his own theoretical principles, Malinowski defined *function* as "the satisfaction of needs by means of an activity in which humans cooperate, use tools and consume merchandise". In order to achieve any objective or attain any goal, humans needed to organise themselves. Organisation implied a very defined schema or structure, the principle elements of which were universal in that they were applicable to all organised groups, and Malinowski proposed giving these units or human organisation the name *institution* (Malinowki, 1944:45). He listed the elements comprising an institution:the charter, the material apparatus, the rules, the activities and, lastly, the function (*Ibíd.*:53).

According to his thesis, the distinguishing elements were the charter and the function. He defined the charter of an institution as a system of values which humans could only achieve through organising themselves or incorporating into existing organisations. He defined "the human element of an institution as the group regulated by precise principles of authority, division of functions and distribution of privileges and duties". He continued, "these consist of the rules or standards of an institution, the technical skills acquired, the habits, the legal precepts or the ethical mandates that are accepted by the members or which are imposed on them" (*Ibíd.*:59).

It is true that some of the meanings he gave to the concept of institution throughout his work, for example, "to highlight the ideal units for establishing comparisons between tribes", were rather unfortunate, and Audrey Richards (1974:33) argued that as a unit, the institution was too big and was composed of too many variables to be handled successfully. Likewise, Malinowski did not appear to distinguish between primary institutions such as the family or chiefdom, and associations of people brought together by common aims, such as a union or a church. These criticisms seem justified when the series of institutions Malinowski considered universal (shown in Table 5) are examined in detail.

Another key problem was his classification of institutions. This did not display the biological focus that he had argued in his theory of needs, since of the seven categories he proposed, only two were primarily biological:'reproduction' and what he called 'biological', which referred to age and sex as criteria for social differentiation (points 1 and 3, respectively, of Table 5). The other five were completely unrelated to biological aspects. This classification, which according to Parsons (1974:72) constituted a good basis for analysis of social structure, since he claimed that was Malinowski's most important theoretical contribution, was rapidly abandoned by Malinowski himself in favour of another question, never to be revisited.

Malinowski was totally explicit in his conviction that the primary aspect of his concept of function was precisely this theory of needs: "It seems clear to me" he said, "that any theory of culture must be based on the organic needs of man, and if it can relate these to more the complex and indirect, but perhaps fully imperative, needs of the kind we call spiritual, economic or social, then it will provide us with the set of general laws that we need from a solid scientific theory" (Malinowksi, 1944:72-73).

However, even if we concede, as Parsons (1974:75) remarked, that Malinowski's classification of cultural responses exhibits a satisfactory relationship with an equally satisfactory classification of basic needs, what remains clear is that this did not help him to construct a bridge over the abyss which separated his concept of basic needs from his own classification of institutions.

Table 5: Types of institution

Principle of integration	Types of institutions
1. REPRODUCTION (blood ties defined by a legal contract of matrimony and later extended by a specifically determined principle of descent in the genealogical schema).	The family, defined as the domestic group of parents and offspring. Organisation of courtship. Legal definition and organisation of matrimony as a contract which unites two individuals and two groups. The extended domestic group and its legal, economic and religious organisation. Kinship groups linked by the unilateral principle of descendants. The matrilineal or patrilineal clan. The system of related clans.
2. TERRITORY (community of interests due to the proximity, availability and possibility of cooperation)	Neighbouring groups, such as the nomadic horde, the locally roaming band, the village or the collection of hamlets and inhabited areas, the town and the city. The district, the province (see nº 7).

3. BIOLOGICAL PRINCIPLE (distinctions due to sex, age and bodily stigmas and symptoms).	Primitive sexual totemic group. Organisation based on physiological or anatomical sexual differences. Organisation based on sexual division of functions and activities. Age groups and degrees, wherever these are organised. In primitive organisations, the organisation of abnormal, mentally degenérate or epileptic individuals (related to religious or magical ideas), or at higher cultural levels, institutions for the ill, insane, or those with congenital defects.
4. VOLUNTARY ASSOCIATIONS	Primitive secret societies, leisure facilities and artistic societies. At the highest level of culture, clubs, charitable and mutual assistance societies, voluntary associations for leisure, moral education or achieving a common goal.

| 5. OCCUPATIONS AND PROFESSIONS. (The organisation of human beings according to specialised activities on the basis of common interests or goals, in order to exploit their particular aptitudes). | On a primitive level, principally sorcerers, witches, shamans and priests; also crafts guilds and economic groups. In more developed civilisations, the innumerable trades, guilds and groups arising around economic interest; professional associations in the fields of medicine, law, education and priesthood. Also, institutions specific to the organised practice of teaching (schools, colleges, universities); for research (laboratorios, academies, institutes); for the administration of justice (legislative bodies, tribunes, poice force); for religion (parishes, sects, churches). |

6. RANK AND STATUS.	Ranks and levels of nobility, clergy, bourgeoisie, peasents, serfs and slaves. The Caste system. Ethnic stratification:racial and cultural distinctions in primitive and developed civilisations.
7. INCLUSIVE PRINCIPLE or COMPREHENSIVE INTEGRATION. (community intergation of culture or political power).	The tribe as the cultural unit corresponding to nationalidad at higher levels. The cultural sub-group formed by geographical location or membership of insular communities (foreign minorities, ghettos, gypsies). The political unit which may comprise part or the totality of the tribe, and may include various cultural sub-divisions. The distinction between tribe-nation and tribe-state as political organisation is fundamental.

Source:Malinowski, 1984:83-85.

From this series of bases and principles, Malinowski (1944:159-160) argued various general axioms of functionalism in his analysis of culture, which merely repeated ideas that he had already presented:

- Culture is essentially an instrumental heritage by which man is situated in the best position to solve the concrete and specific problems which arise in his surroundings, during the course of satisfying his needs.
- It is a system of objects, activities and attitudes in which each part exists as a menas to an end.
- It is an integrated set in which the various elements are independent.
- These activities, attitudes and objects are organised around important and vital tasks in institutions such as the family, the clan, the local community, the tribe and the organisational groups for economic cooperation and political, legal and educational activities.
- From a dynamic point of view, that is to say, with reference to the type of activity, culture can be analysed according to a certian number of aspects such as educaion, social control, the economy, knowledge, belief and morality systems, and even methods of artistic and creative expression.

In addition to the criticisms mentioned earlier, there were others which questioned the validity of this analysis as a general basis for understanding human behaviour in cultures and as a conceptual tool for observing and collecting data. One such criticism, for example, concerned the terminology, given that the multiple denominations that Malinowski used for needs led to confusion. Another question was the exact definition of the different needs and the minimum conditions necessary for their satisfaction. As Piddington (1974:53 and ss.) remarked, a further question was to what extent integrative imperatives such as determined forms of art, ceremony or leisure could be considered necessary for biological survival in the same way that nutrition or reproduction were, even though they had a physiological basis in terms of enjoyment of cetain kinds of sensory impression (visual, auditory and even olfactory and gustatory). Nevertheless, this same author found an operative relevance in the theory of needs, since it provided a means of organising and analysing the data collected by an ethnographer, in so far as these are generally cultural responses to derived or integrative needs, and above all, since it functioned as a satisfactory guide for new field researchers: "As is natural, a student prepared according to this programme would not be qualified to carry out ethnographic research, but in the vast majority of cases, however, this is not what students go on to do. For the rare exceptions to this rule, specialisation can come afterwards".

The theory also provided a "basis for cooperation between psychologists and anthropologists" in that it made it possible to demonstrate the several ways in which different cultures address the raw material of human nature. In other words, psychologists concern themselves with the impulses and motivations of individuals, whether these are common to a group or purely individual, and the context in which these impulses operate is taken as given. In contrast, anthropologists are interested in the organisation in itself of these institutions, and in the "routine organisation of satisfaction" (or frustration).

Paradoxically, this link between anthropology and psychology contributed, to a large extent, to the abandonment of the theory of needs by anthropologists, due to "the resistence of British social anthropologists to psychogical concepts" (Geddes, 1953, quoted by Piddington, 1974:58).

4.2. Perspectives on cultural change

Towards the end of the 1920s, Malinowski became interested in the issue of cultural change, and the development of a 'practical anthropology' as a research tool. From then until 1942, he published a series of articles on this subject which were subsequently put in order by Phyllis Kaberry and published posthumously together with other materials in 1945, in a book entitled *The Dynamics of Culture Change*.

Although Malinowski acted in the capacity of expert on numerous occasions, and paid a four month visit in 1934 to his disciples working in Africa with societies in the process of rapid change, his perspective of time indicated that he lacked the experience required for field work in this context. Consequently, his approach has been described as 'schematic and exploratory'. However, I will examine it from the perspective of the period in which it was developed.

His theory on culture change, as shown in Figure 6, could not be generalised to all situations but rather referred to the impact of industrialisation on peasant societies. For his examples he used the field work that his disciples were conducting in Africa. He remarked that "culture change in Africa does not differ in essence from that which is currently transforming rural and backward European countries, converting peasant communities into a new kind of community extremely similar to the proletariat found in industrial districts of the United States, England or France"

(Malinowski, 1945:2). This opinion gained ground and, as Lucy Mair (1974:255) commented, for a while much research was conducted in rural communities in France, Spain, Turkey and America applying methods which were no more than an extension of Malinowski's own.

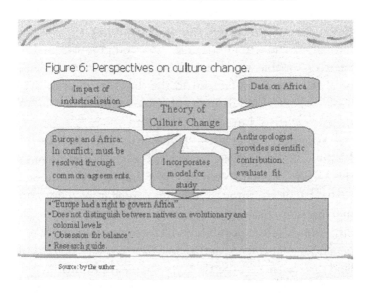

Figure 6: Perspectives on culture change.

Source: by the author

The scope of his generalisations was limited by the fact that his African material came from societies subject to political domination by European governments or by immigrant communities from Europe. His analytical method was based on a tabular schema which guaranteed, according to Malinowski himself (1945:32), the recording of all pertinent facts and the clarification of all the connections between them. It presented the contributions of the two cultures in contact using various columns, one for the 'imperialist power' and the other for the 'colonial subjects': between these Malinowski inserted another column for the 'new cultural reality' which resulted from their interaction. These he correlated using a large number of entries, among which featured a series of prohibitions and other aspects which he grouped together under the epigraph 'surviving forms of tradition'.

However, as Radcliffe-Brown has made a point of emphasising, Malinowski reduced the question to a mere clash between African and European institutions, rendering individual and group struggles and compromises in the heart of variable social structures an abstraction. In fact, he always remained faithful to the theory that 'primitive' societies had existed in a state of stable equilibrium prior to the emergence of European colonialism.

According to Harris (1987:481), the essence of Malinowski's theory of change was that the Europeans and the Africans were involved in a 'give and take' that needed to be balanced through the development of 'common measures' or commitment to 'tasks of mutual interest'. In order to assess the possibilities of these peaceful, mutually beneficial adjustments, anthropologists would be obliged to lend their scientific expertise to the colonial administrations by examining the entire cultural context of the institutions and the African and European alternatives. Anthropologists should assume the task of conducting this analysis, making a special effort not to conceal any fact related to the failure on the part of Europeans to give the Africans as much as the former had taken from them, whilst at the same time taking care not to succumb "to an outburst of pro-native indignation". In other words, anthropologists should be governed by the principles of moderation, commitment and decorum (Malinowski, 1945:58). But he did not address the question of why the Africans, the invaded and exploited, should give the Europeans anything in return. Malinowski's basic premise was that the Europeans had a right to govern the African, and that to be fair, any future settlement would have to give European interests the part that by law and custom corresponded to them. Thus at one point he asserted that "where there is effective cooperation (between whites and blacks), a new form of social organisation is generated:a native African Christian congregation guided and supervised by a white clergy; a superintended mine or factory with black labour managed by white staff; a native administrative system under European control. In this way, the results of the impact would not form disorganised facts, but rather the new institutions (. . .) would respond to European plans, ideas and needs whilst at the same time satisfying some African needs" (*Ibíd.*:65).

In this respect, Malinowski never totally achieved the capacity to distinguish between the natives as primitives in an evolutionary order and natives as primitives in a Euro-American colonial order. Malinowski's assertion quoted by Harris (*Ibíd.*) is significant here: "the practical value of a theory such as this (functionalism) is that of showing us the relative importance of the diverse customs, the ways in which they are assembled and how they should be treated by missionaries, the colonial authorities and those whose mission it is to economically exploit the trade and work of the savages".

It is regarding this aspect that the theory was most strongly criticised, particularly by Max Gluckman. Gluckman (1947:109 and ss.) asserted that Malinowski was incapable of liberating himself from the functionalist insistence on equilibrium: "his system of instrumental needs can only explain how tensions and conflicts are mitigated or eliminated, but not how or why they originate nor how or why they intensify Thus, instead or producing a theory of change, all that he achieved was to broaden his theory of no-change". And he continued, "Malinowski could not include conflict in his schema of integrated institutions and concern himself with conflict as an inherent attribute of social organisation'. Malinowski's only conceptual mechanism (and that of Gluckman, as he himself recognised and as did many others who wrote about conflict during this period) was that provided by Durkheim, which established that despite the existence of conflict, social solidarity was always maintained.

4.3. Field work in Mexico

In 1940, two years after arriving in the United States on a one year sabbatical, Malinowski commenced a new project in Mexico. He proposed to analyse the Zapotec market system in Oaxaca. Together with the Mexican researcher Julio de la Fuente, he proposed a series of studies on this subject and conducted two periods of field work in the summers of 1940 and 1941. The result of this collaboration was the book ***The Economics of a Mexican Market System***, published in 1957, fifteen years after it had originally been written.

As Aguirre Beltrán observed, once a social agitator, Julio de la Fuente had became a social researcher and analyst, and had just finished writing the first draft of his monograph on *Yalalag, una villa zapoteca serrana* (*Yalalag, a Zapotec mountain village*), which would not be published until 1949. He participated in the project as an associate researcher under the direction of Malinowski.

Malinowski had selected the Oaxaca Valley in part because "no other ethnographer had been there before him", in part because it was the centre of an important archaeological dig directed by Dr. Alfonso Caso, at Monte Albán, but above all because it presented a wide variety of historical, ethnographic and 'practical' problems. However, the truth was that this area was not unknown to other ethnographers, and had even been studied more than other parts of Mexico. Thus, for example, Malinowski acknowledged that he had found the work of E. C. Parsons on Mitla, published in 1936, useful, although he did not like the approach described:he felt that the attempt to distinguish between what was 'Indian' and what was 'Spanish' was too historical.

Another important precedent in anthropological studies in Mexico was the monumental report by Manuel Gamio (a disciple of F. Boas), on San Juan de Teotihuacan, to the north of Mexico City and published in 1922. Although Malinowski, who had met Gamio on his first visit to Mexico in 1926, was not impressed by the latter's perspective on the *survivals* he identified in this culture, he was however interested in the data Gamio provided about this community in terms of how it tackled 'progress' since this was the type of 'practical' problem which interested him.

In contrast, he was more sympathetic to the work of Redfield in Tepoztlan, or that which the latter was conducting with Alfonso Villa Roja in Yucatán. But by choosing the Oaxaca Valley, he had selected a geographically and culturally different area to the Morelos Valley or the Yucatán peninsula, which is where Redfield was working. Additionally, whereas Redfield's studies centred on a variety of aspects of the social life of a single community, Malinowski wished to examine the inter-relationships created between several communities by a single institution, in this case the market. Despite the foregoing, his work was presented as a contribution to the ethnography of Mexico, as was that of Manuel Gamio, Robert Redfield and Alfonso Villa Rojas, following the example that they had set.

The book had a two-fold purpose, that of serving as an educational tool showing field work procedures, and that of presenting a study of the market system which addressed the question "What is the function of the numerous small markets spread throughout the Oaxaca Valley"?

As regards the first aim, Malinowski intended that the book should serve as educational material. At the time, particular interest was being shown within Mexican anthropology and, more specifically, the recently created Indigenist Institute (1940), in this issue. The work of Redfield and Gamio contributed little to field work techniques. Gamio's work was to a large extent historical and rather conjectural, whilst that of Redfield provided a series of data collected through observation, and descriptions of the day to day behaviour of people, but never referred to the methods used.

A comparison with Malinowski's other works arises spontaneously since he himself frequently referred to them throughout the text, and the question of method is simply another aspect of this. Thus, although he did not use analogies with the laboratory experiments of natural science as he had done in *Argonauts*, when discussing field work he did emphasise that the way in which questions are formulated should arise from 'the natural observation of acts' and that generalisations should be made "on the basis of field research, based on the facts observed and not on armchair conjecture" (Malinowski & De la Fuente, 1957:188). When defining determined concepts, he referred to his previous publications, principally *Argonauts*, *Coral Gardens* and *Culture* (Malinowski, 1922, 1935 and 1931, respectively), and consequently the theoretical content did not offer any significant novelty. He emphasised a little more the concepts of 'charter' and 'function' in terms of how "they served him to construct his thesis from the observed data". "The functionalist approach", he said (Malinowski & De la Fuente, 1957:183), "presupposes the existence of certain general principles", and stressed again that "these generalisations should be constructed on the basis of meticulously observed data, and formulated inductively with reference to the culture as a whole".

In contrast to the Trobriand Islands, which he had presented as a culturally homogeneous region, the Oaxaca Valley was an area of extreme cultural diversity and he acknowledged that due to the complexity of the social structures involved, a complete study of the market systems, which would form part of a global study of the national economy, went beyond the competence of an ethnographer, and that he would consequently require the cooperation of specialists in other disciplines. Money was used in the market, together with different kinds of weights and measures, and much of the study dealt with these issues. Nevertheless, there were similarities between the Trobriand Islanders and those frequenting the Oaxaca markets. From outside, the impression they gave (*Ibid.:*82 and ss.) was that of a series of neighbouring villages which were economically interdependent within the same region:those in the Mixteca Highlands to the north and west, and those in the Zapotec Highlands to the south and east. These villages and towns, as dispersed throughout Oaxaca as the Trobriand communities were throughout the archipelago, were linked through a system of exchange. However, in contrast to the Trobriand communities, in Oaxaca these exchanges were brief and finite, and the resulting institution was much more complex. Malinowski's detailed description of the exchanges, given in chapter 8, frequently recalls the exchanges he had described in other books. Further on in the book, he focused more on the question of social change, a theme to which he had made scant reference in his works on the Trobriand Islands.

Whilst in these he had presented an economic analysis in which he described individuals guided by the law of minimum effort, in his economic analysis of Oaxaca he presented individuals motivated by utilitarianism. The

Oaxaca natives went to the market for business reasons and not for any other collateral reason: "our final conclusion is that the market is almost exclusively an economic market in the conception and ideas of the natives themselves. (. . .) Nobody goes to the market except with the purpose to buy or sell" (*Ibíd.*:189). Thus, it would seem that he accepted the perspective of the natives with regard to the nature of the market, as a simply utilitarian exchange. However, he also observed that other important questions were involved, such as those which emerged during local and national festivities for patron saints, the 'mayordomías' (*Ibíd.*:110), when the markets were full of objects such as flowers votive offerings, scapulars, prayers written on cards, baskets filled with medicinal herbs for offerings, candles, etc., which were no more utilitarian than the objects exchanged in the *kula*.

Malinowski and De la Fuente also discussed the 'psychology of the market' (*Ibíd.*:189) in relation to the preference for buying at the market instead of in shops, due to the manner in which the transactions were conducted.

Among the different categories of people who participated in the market, whether as seller or buyer, they observed (*Ibíd.*:108 and ss.) that many people performed both roles, acting as the seller in one transaction and then changing role to act as buyer in another. This led the authors to one of their most interesting observations, that of the market as a reserve or 'tractable bank', always available and accessible. In turn, this led them to discuss the role of the reseller and the hoarder and their influence on the market and on fixing prices.

Malinowksi and De la Fuente (*Ibíd.*:116) highlighted the importance of production and consumption patterns, which comprised the basic elements for understanding the market system. However, they also indicated the great need for subsequent studies on land ownership and agricultural production in order to arrive at a full understanding of the system. Lastly, they observed that the problem with their suggestion that the market functioned primarily as an economic mechanism was "how to draw the line between economic and non-economic activities". Without entering into a full theoretical discussion, they expressed their conviction that "the best way to approach this problem from an ethnographic point of view is to define as economic any activity which is connected to the processes of production, distribution and consumption of goods" (*Ibíd.*:190).

The questions that they addressed in the book, together with the overall context of the markets, provided an impression of social life in the Oaxaca Valley. Thus, *The Economics of a Mexican Market System* can be considered as a further contribution by Malinowski to the discipline of anthropology. The subjects were not new, as they had already appeared throughout his writings, but the novelty lay in the ethnographic sphere addressed, which was totally new for Malinowski, and the fact that it was produced towards the end of his career and life. The book indisputably forms part of the history of ethnographic research on Oaxaca, and played a prominent role in the development of anthropology in Mexico.

4.4. A question of style

There is one aspect of Malinowski's work that has aroused the interest of other disciplines outside anthropology, which is that of rhetoric and the literary style of his work. The way in which he constructed his monographs was yet another innovative contribution. Most of the studies which have addressed this aspect, with the exception of what is perhaps the most significant one, that of Payne (1981), have focused on *Argonauts of the Western Pacific* as a paradigmatic example of an ethnographic text. However, any of his writings could equally serve for an analysis of this kind. Even in his earliest works, such as *The Natives of Mailu*, it is possible to detect some of the rhetorical and stylistic features of his later works, which were more detailed and better constructed. The richness of Malinowski's ethnographic experience on the Trobriand Islands permeates the text of *Argonauts*, and he used it as a narrative resource to the extent that, as Young (1988:33) observed, the Trobriand Islanders' *kula* journey became, by extension, a metaphor for his own excellent but labyrinthine journey of discovery.

In addition to his literary qualities as a passionate narrator, evidenced in his descriptions of the landscape, the *kula*, the life cycle or the agricultural year, Payne (1981:422) remarked that Malinowski's style took two forms:a strictly narrative style and a moralistic one. Apparently opposites, the two forms are also linked, and show a similarity to two others ways of being, as established by Geertz (1988:79 and ss.):the first is that of the 'absolute cosmopolitan', a figure with an enhanced capacity to adapt to any situation without losing a sense of self whilst being at the same time capable of seeing as the savages saw, thinking and speaking as they felt and believed, and even on occasions, feeling as they felt and thinking as they thought. The other figure is that of the researcher, demonstrating rigorous objectivity, dispassionate, meticulous, fair, disciplined and dedicated, in sum, a figure in pursuit of the truth. Thus he conveyed his 'scientific heroism', showing and even making readers feel that he was on the point of discovering something that hitherto had never seen before.

In addition, Malinowski dramatised some of his experiences in the field, turning them into ethnographhic data and thus demonstrating how his own interaction could generate valuable information. On this aspect, Geertz

(1967:12) observed that these anecdotes could be read as fables about *rapport*, of the 'harmonious relationship' indispensable for confirming the 'ethnographic authority' discussed by Geertz himself (1988:76), clearly declaring "I was there" although the primary goal was to adorn and embellish the ethnographic aspect. Malinowski first experimented with this technique in *The Natives of Mailu* (Malinowski, 1915:269, 300, 306, to give some examples). Perhaps the most paradigmatic case I have identified is precisely in this same study, when Malinowski took part in negotiations between Igua, his cook Motuan, and Pikana, a Mailu man who wanted to sell a special stone to Igua as part of his dugong (*Dugong dugon*) magic. Malinowski played the devil's advócate, persuading Igua not to buy the stone as Pikana would cheat him and give him a false stone:in this way he could avoid the danger of having his magic robbed and at the same time would not lose his money. Igua withdrew from the negotiations and thus saved his money. In this instance, Malinowski left the reader to ponder the ethics of his 'experimental' intervention. The device of showing 'us' as ethnographically distant from 'the Other' is rhetorically effective and became one of Malinowski's favourite ploys.

The methodological justification for this kind of 'experimentation' certainly canot be applied to the following example, also taken from *Mailu*: "I returned at night, once again with a scared boy I call Monkey. He appeared to have heard some strange noises and was very frightened. I told him to follow me, offering him tobacco in an attempt to convince him. Suddenly I hid and he started to scream" (Malinowski, 1915:246-7). More than an example of ethnographical authority, this would appear to be an example of bad taste and a tiresome sense of humour.

It was through this kind of rhetorical style that Malinowski expressed his stance towards the natives and towards other issues such as colonialism. I have remarked that he experimented with this style in *Mailu* because later, similar examples appeared in ***A Diary in the Strict Sense of the Term*** (Malinowski, 1967), although not in *Argonauts* or *Coral Gardens*.

His *Diary*, discovered shortly after his death but not published until some years later, is a crucial document in the history of anthropology. Here, he demonstrated the style previously dubbed 'being there', in what has been called 'Conradian terms'. If, as Firth (1974 a:7) claimed, he had expressed the ambition to become 'the Conrad of anthropology', with his *Diary* it would appear that he achieved his desire.

The *Diary* presents us with the problem that all anthropologists face in their field work:loneliness, the struggle with a physically and culturally different environment, the test of character that this difference represents, etc. Paradoxically, these are the themes that appear in Joseph Conrad's novel *Heart of Darkness* (1902). Like Malinowski, this novelist was Polish, and they shared a similar life history, united by historical contingencies and living out their respective careers in England. As he tells us in his *Diary*, Malinowski read his novels.

Both *Heart of Darkness* and the *Diary* portray a crisis of identity, 'the struggle on the limits of civilisation' and a moral defeat which leads to a profound psychological crisis. The experiences that Malinowski described in his *Diary* depict this 'emotional and spiritual crisis' and in the same way that in *Heart of Darkness* Marlow defends his life and his steam boat in the heart of Africa, so Malinowski clung to the routine of his work, urging himself to remain focused and continue working, concentrating on the goal that had led him 'there' (Malinowski, 1967:168).

For these reasons, the *Diary* can to some extent be considered a crucial document in the history of anthropology, not because it depicts the reality of the ethnographer's experience but because it confronts us with the complexity of such an experience:the sensation of confinement, the tedium experienced by the solitary researcher, the longing for family, colleagues and friends, the fear of illnesss, the tiredness, the sexual frustration, the tantrums when the post does not arrive or the natives show scant signs of cooperation, the irritations caused by field work, the obsession with returning to one's own cultural environment even though "only for a moment", as Firth described in the introduction to the book.

For Malinowski himself, his personal diary was a safety valve, and as his students remarked on several occasions according to Kuper (1973:28), "a means of channelling the personal concerns and emotions of the ethnographer, separately from his scientific notes".

Through his *Diary*, Malinowski showed what Stocking (1968:192 and ss.) called an 'intellectual humanism' worthy of regard, not only for his unique personality but also for his mental and intellectual wealth. It was an explicit attempt to reveal the internal dynamics of his mind, and this he uncovered, to a large extent, through reflecting on and admitting the darker sides of his nature. Thus, writing a diary may have been a precondition for his own survival at the heart of ethnographic work. It was his internal enclave of European culture, and at the same time his particular form of internal communication. It was what enabled him to maintain the 'empathy' that we have historically associated with anthropological field work.

Despite the controversy aroused by publication due to the quantity of pages devoted to expressing his rage, his sexual frustration and his hysteria, the fact is that the *Diary* presents the two opposed poles of all the criticisms directed at Malinowski:on the one hand, "the struggle of a man such as Malinowski, in a hostile environment, to maintain his identity as an individual and as a member of a culture" (Forge, 1967:222), and on the other, "his arrogance and supremacy", his "hypochondria and narcissism", and even his "ethnocentricity" (Geertz, 1967:12). Neither of the perspectives was new, and had already appeared in other books, although perhaps in other terms given the genre in question, namely, a personal diary not intended for publication.

Malinowski's impact was considerable even in this respect, and remains unsurpassed, which is not to say that some have not tried to imítate him. If we were to look for another such benchmark, we would have to wait until the 1955 publication of *Tristes Tropiques* (translated into English as *A World on the Wane*) by Lévi-Strauss, where he continued in what Panoff (1974:92) called "the glorious tradition of a philosophical journey and in which he would fruitlessly seek what constituted the paradox of Malinowski:the success of a scientific work through the mechanisms characteristic of literary creation"

Indeed, even here Malinowski exercised an influence, establishing a new style, a particular way of writing a monograph. This has been acknowledged in several studies on the subject concerning the now classic works of his disciples and detractors and mentioned in the book *Writing Culture* by James Clifford and George E. Marcus.

The last aspect of Malinowski's style and rhetoric refers to the role his companion and wife, Elsie Masson Malinowskova, played in his writings, considered by some fundamental. Documents exist corroborating her role in his literary output, which to a certain extent had already been assumed. Raymond Firth (1981:107) attested to her 'good taste' and 'good, critical mind'. He also described how she spent much time reading and discussing Malinowski's work, and the high value the latter placed on his wife's criticisms.

Elsie had published a book herself in 1915, an account of a year she had spent in wild country in the north of Australia (*An Untamed Territory*). Helena Wayne (1984:198), their youngest daughter, has revealed that her father was impressed by his wife's book. Shortly after meeting but before they became engaged, he asked for her help with his work, and their collaboration was promptly cemented. In *Baloma*, Malinowski did not refer to or acknowledge her help although it "was at that time", in 1915, "that such cooperation began". "It was above all during their first year of marriage, which they spent in Melbourne, and the following, in the Canary Islands, that he wrote *Argonauts* and Elsie acted as helpmeet, critic and much more, and not only as regards his style". again, in *Argonauts* Malinowski did not refer to his wife's help, and she was not acknowledged until *The sexual life of savages*, where he wrote at the end of the prologue: "I owe a great debt in this book, as in all those I have written, to my wife. Her advice and practical cooperation transformed the difficult task of writing *Argonauts* and the present book into an agreeable one. If for me, personally, there is any value or interest in these works, it is due to the part she played in a shared task" (Malinowski, 1929:48). Later, he dedicated *Coral Gardens* to her, saying, again at the end of the prologue: "I believe that this is the best book I have written and that I will probably ever write. In this and other aspects of my research, her critical advice and suggestions have been a more valuable and effective inspiration than I can say" (Malinowski, 1935:22), despite the fact that, as Wayne (*Ibíd.*) remarked, "it was the book in which she collaborated least because, during its writing, she was already suffering from multiple sclerosis, and she did not live to see it in print."

However, Elsie Masson Malinowska contributed so much to his works on the Trobriand Islands, and wielded such great influence on his literary style, that she even chose his tropes, wording and metaphors. Nevertheless, Clifford (1986) suggested that Malinowski was also impressed with his own, unassisted writing, without the help of his wife, perhaps because "he would never have imagined that the wife of Joseph Conrad had played a similar role in his literary production".

5. AN EVALUATION OF MALINOWSKI

To briefly summarise Malinowski's theoretical contribution, his achievement in introducing several subjects which would become recurring themes in the subsequent development of anthroppology must be acknowledged. With his inspired intuition, he broached a mass of ideas which later served as the working hypotheses for numerous anthropologists, and were explored in detail and disseminated by the best minds. examples of this would be his recommendation concerning the use of the vernacular language, not only as a tool for improving data collection but also for improving relationships with the people and achieving a better understanding of their society and culture, or his inspired insistence on the totality, which rendered *Argonauts of the Western Pacific* a work of art. On this point, Panoff (1974:87 and ss.) observed that it was of little importance if later he took the wrong path or his studies provided a mishmash of encyclopaediac data instead of brilliant insights, since his message had already been understood and was being successfully implemented. Thus, Marcel Mauss would develop Malinowski's theoretical implications further, giving them a wider audience. Even today, when there is a tendency in the discipline towards segmentation into specialised areas which guard their autonomy jealously, the concept of totality continues to inspire the most important works of modern times, and Lévi-Strauss is the clearest example of this. But it is not the moment to explain the transcendence of these anthropologists.

Malinowski also contributed to knowledge of 'primitive' economies, both in the way he posed the problem and in the methodological hypotheses he proposed as necessary to arrive at the solution. In this respect, Mauss once again contributed much to clarifying the problem. For example, the concepts of reciprocity and redistribution emerged in debates on the subject, and established the criteria for the analysis of economic systems conducted by Polanyi, who acknowledged that his thoughts in *Trade and Market in the Early Empires* were inspired by the *kula* exchange system. Likewise, Dalton, whose research focused on 'primitive money', took as his point of departure Malinowski's observations, whilst the discussions of Firth and Salisbury on the concept of 'value', in the economic sense of the word, were also stimulated by *Argonauts*.

One field in which his work initially proved to be sterile was that of kinship, where he had not hesitated to express his disdain for what he called the "ridiculous algebra of kinship", namely, the analysis of kinship terminology. In this respect successive intellectual fashions would extol that which he had disregarded or criticised, and he was dismissed as "a sage with no discernment, given to taking one step forwards and two steps back". After Malinowski and under the influence of Radcliffe-Brown, these studies focused on the formal aspects of kinship, such as legal and terminological characteristics (Malinowski had focused his studies on psychological aspects), and thus the discipline of ethnography reinforced its scientific credentials with aridity and technicalities. It should be noted here that, in the words of George Homans (1941:172), "the study of the theories of Malinowski and Racliffe-Brown illustrate a very common feature in scientific controversy:two distinguished personalities who, instead of attempting to find common ground for discussion, speak without listening to each other, presenting their theories as alternatives when in reality they are complementary" (quoted by Harris, 1987:481).

Furthermore, increased ethnological research in Africa demonstrated the capital importance of the political role of wider kinship groups (clans and lineages) and their process of segmentation, providing a different direction to that of Malinowski, who preferred to limit research to inter-individual relationships, and in particular to the nuclear or conjugal family. This opened him to accusations of ethnocentricity, and of having transposed the prototypcal European bourgeoise family to the tropics.

However, refinements to the "algebra of kinship" resulting from new intellectual fashions led to a dazzling rehabilitation of Malinowski over two stages, as observed by Panoff (1974:90), with two categories of argument, one of a comparative nature and the other concerning logic. Firstly, the compilation of data on 250 different societies led Murdock (1949) to confirm the universal and central nature of the nuclear family as an institution with a distinctive physiognomy. Secondly, the examination of kinship terminologies using componential analysis, which combines modern semantic methods with formal logic, led Lounsbury (1965) to conclude that the results obtained indirectly demonstrated the validity, or at least the fertility, of Malinowski's 'extensionalist' theory (the same word denominates kin of a very different degree. The name given to the closest kin, the mother, was extended to more distant kin, the mother's brother, her cousins, etc., who adopted the same attitude with regard to the child. This psychological progression helped the child to discover the individuals who belonged to his or her social circle).

Another noteworthy aspect is that those who have devoted themselves to a consideration of the practical problems and methods involved in field work have done so on the basis of identical experiences to those of Malinowski, and even sometimes using the same terminology. And so I could go on, discussing other themes.

However, if the aim is to arrive at something like a general consensus among social anthropologists regarding Malinowski's place in the discipline's history, it is probable that such agreement would be focused mainly on the excellent quality of his observations in the field and on his contribution to the development of field work techniques, together with his contribution to training an entire generation of ethnologists.

Evidently, for most of us, functionalism in the terms that Malinowski conceived of it has become unacceptable. The theoretical proposal that he constructed over 15 years has been shown to be incapable of "supporting the systematic weight that he wanted it to bear". However, much of his theory is still useful, and has inspired abundant ideas in others, who often have not acknowledged the source of their inspiration. The fervour with which, in his times, functionalism was received by an elite intellectual circle, Leach said (1974:297) was closely linked to Malinowski's personality, as he "had many of the qualities of a prophet, was a charismatic leader, conscious of his powers and his grandeur. He saw himself as an innovator, revolutionising the field of methodology and anthropological ideas who underrated the importance of his more conservative contemporaries and his immediate predeccesors. He presented himself as the creator of a completely new discipline, to the extent that an entire generation of disciples was educated in the belief that social anthropology began in 1914 on the Trobriand Islands.

Retrospectively however, the brilliant creator would seem to be quite similar to his more conventional contemporaries. In this, the same occurred with Malinowski in social anthropology as can be seen to have happened with any great figure of a scientific discipline. Whilst we might think that he originated a 'new era' in anthropology, it should be recognised that he was a scholar who came to maturity in the first decades of the 20th century and was consequently a child of his times, sharing without hesitation most of the prejudices held by those of his generation and was even a victim of the epistemological prejudices that he himself so bravely attacked. In this respect, Leach (1974:312) stated: "Malinowski was thwarted by the persistence of his youthful intellectual prejudices, and this would probably apply to us as well. I have emphasised", Leach continued, "that Malinowski was bound to his predeccesors:he rebelled against them because his debt to them was so great. Perhaps this is also the case for some of us with Bronislaw Malinowski".

But it would be absurd to suggest that Malinowski's intellectual endeavours had remained at an eternal standstill in his times; on the contrary, he can be considered the precursor of many fields within anthropology. Indisputably, field work was never the same after the publication of *Argonauts of the Western Pacific.* Harris (1978:473) has stated that Malinowski's ethnological contributions have never yet been surpassed by anyone. His monographs on the Trobriand Islands contintue to constitute the greatest ethnographic description yet written. And although he has been described as a mediocre theoretician because some of his theories have not stood the test of time or have been shown to possess evident imperfections, perhaps his greatest contribution was not in his specific theories but in his insistence on the need for theory, the relating of the particular to the general, in all stages of anthropological research.

Certainly, his entire legacy has been the subject of heated controversy, as with any substantial inheritance. However, although his discourse on culture and the functional cohesion of societies is less widely read now than before, his legacy has been accepted and the most original and important aspects of it have been understood and assimilated.

During the Second World War and in the final years of his life, spent in the United States, Malinowski wrote **Freedom and Civilisation** (Malinowski, 1947), a 'hymn to freedom', a book in which, apart from being a surprising marriage between his funcionalist theory and a universalist variety of evolutionsim, showed his frank political commitment. The brutal consequences of the war would seem to have awakened in him a new interest in the Polish cause. His wife commented that the invasion of Poland caused a deep impression on him, and seemed to awaken his hitherto dormant nationalist sentiment and feelings of solidarity with the Poles. He took an active part in founding the Polish Institute and in assisting exiled Polish scholars. It was a way to support the cause which to him seemed to be that of liberty and civilisation, and of attacking totalitarianism and Nazism, although his reactions were more those of an intellectual than of a politician.

Malinowski died in 1942. In his obituary of James Frazer, his mentor, he had written "the death of Frazer symbolises the end of an era". Perhaps the same could be said of Malinowski. Functionalism had formed the foundation on which he raised the edifice of British Social Anthropology. In the period immediately following the Seond World War, structuralism gained such a firm foothold that there was almost no time left to evaluate functionalism on its own terms. I hope that this lesson will serve to remedy this to some extent.

6. REFERENCES

ÁLVAREZ MUNARRIZ, L., (2001) 'La configuración cultural de la sexualidad en B. Malinowski', Gorka (ed.) *La sexualidad humana*, Murcia, Godoy, cap. 2.

ÁLVAREZ ROLDAN, A., (1994) 'La invención del método etnográfico. Reflexiones sobre el trabajo de campo de Malinowski en Melanesia'. *Antropología*, 7:83-100.

BESTARD I CAMPS, J., (1993) 'Malinowski:entre Kraków e Icod. El modernismo polaco y las etnografías modernistas', en Bestard i Camps, J. (coord.) *Después de Malinowski*. Tenerife, FAAEE, pp. 7-31.

BESTARD I CAMPS, J., (1995) 'Els orígens polonesos de l'empirisme de Malinowski', prólogo a *Malinowswki* (1995) Barcelona, Icaria, pp. 9-29.

CLIFFORD, J., (1985) 'On Ethnographic self-Fashioning:Conrad and Malinowki', in T.C. Heller, M. Sosna, & D. E. Wellbery (eds.) *Reconstructing Individualism.* California, Stanford University Press, pp. 93-113.

CLIFFORD, J. & MARCUS, G. E., (eds.) (1991) *Retóricas de la Antropología.* Madrid, Júcar.

CONRAD, J., (1902) *El corazón de las tinieblas.* Madrid, Alianza, 1986.

ELLEN, R., GELLNER, E., KUBICA, G. & MUCHA, J. (ed.). (1988) *Malinowski between two worlds.* Cambridge University Press.

ESTEVA FABREGAT, C. (1965) *Función y Funcionalismo en las Ciencias Sociales.* Madrid, CSIC.

EVANS PRITCHARD, E. E., (1951) *Social Anthropology.* New York, Free Press.

FERNÁNDEZ, O., (1994) 'El estilo de Malinowski en *Los Argonautas del Pacífico Occidental*', *Estudios Humanísticos (Filología),* 16:89-99.

FERNÁNDEZ, O., (1998) 'Conrad y Malinowski en el Corazón de las Tinieblas', *Estudios Humanísticos (Filología),* 20:179-190.

FERNÁNDEZ, O., (2004) *Bronislaw Malinowski:la Antropología y el Funcionalismo.* León, Universidad de León.

FERNÁNDEZ, O., (2012) 'Malinowski And the New Humanism', *History of the Human Sciences,* 25 (2).

FIRTH, J. R. (1974) 'El análisis etnográfico y el lenguaje en la obra de Malinowski', Firth, R., (ed.) *Hombre y cultura. La obra de Bronislaw Malinowski.* Madrid, Siglo XXI, pp.111-140.

FIRTH, R., (1936) *We, the Tikopia:A Sociological Study of Kinship in Primitive Polynesia.* London, Allen & Unwin.

FIRTH, R., (1974 a) 'Introducción:Malinowski como científico y como hombre', en Firth, R., Leach, E., y otros, *Hombre y cultura. La obra de Bronislaw Malinowski.* Madrid, Siglo XXI, pp. 1-17.

FIRTH, R., (1974 b) 'El lugar de Malinowski en la historia de la antropología económica', en Firth, R., Leach, E., y otros, *Hombre y cultura. La obra de Bronislaw Malinowski.* Madrid, Siglo XXI, pp. 227-248.

FIRTH, R., (1981) 'Bronislaw Malinowski', in Selverman, S. (ed.), *Totems and Teachers. Perspectives on the History of Anthropology.* New York, Columbia University Press, cap. 4, pp. 101—139.

FIRTH, R., (1988) 'Malinowski in the history of anthropology', en Ellen, R., Gellner, E., Kubica, G. & Mucha, J. et al. (ed.) *Malinowski Between Two Worlds,* pp.12-42.

FIRTH, R.; LEACH, E., y otros, (1974) *Hombre y cultura. La obra de Bronislaw Malinowski.* Madrid, Siglo XXI.

FLIS, A., (1988) 'Cracow philosophy at the beginning of the twentieth century, and the rise of Malinowski's scientific ideas', en Ellen, R., Gellner, E., Kubica, G. & Mucha, J. et al. (ed.) *Malinowski Between Two Worlds*, pp. 105-127.

FORGE, A., (1967) 'The Lonely Anthropologist', *New Society*, 17:221-223.

FORTES, M., (1974) 'Malinowski y el estudio del parentesco', en en Firth, R., Leach, E., y otros, *Hombre y cultura. La obra de Bronislaw Malinowski*. Madrid, Siglo XXI, pp. 161-200.

FORTUNE, R. F. (1932) *Sorcerers of Dobu*. Londres.

GEERTZ, C. (1967) 'Under the Mosquito Net', *The New York Review of Books*, 14 Sep:12-13.

GEERTZ, C. (1988) 'I-Witnessing. Malinowski's Children', *Works and Lives. The Anthropologist as Author*. Stanford, California, Stanford University Press, pp. 73-101.

GELLNER, E., (1988) 'Zeno of Cracow' or 'Revolution at Nemi' or 'The Polish revenge:a drama in three acts', en Ellen, R., Gellner, E., Kubica, G. & Mucha, J. et al. (ed.) *Malinowski Between Two Worlds*, pp. 164-194.

GLUCKMAN, M., (1947) 'Malinowski's 'functional' analysis of social change', *Africa*, vol. XVII, n.2:103-121.

GLUCKMAN, M., (1965) *Política, derecho y ritual en una sociedad tribal*. Madrid, Akal. 1978.

GODELIER, M., (1972) *Funcionalismo, estructuralismo y marxismo*. Barcelona, Cuadernos Anagrama.

HARRIS, M., (1987) *El desarrollo de la teoría antropológica. Una historia de las teorías de la cultura*. Madrid, Siglo XIX.

HENSON, H. (1974) *British Anthropologists and Language. A History of Separate Development*. Oxford, Clarendon Press.

JERCHINA, J., (1988) 'Polish culture of modernism and Malinowski's personality', en Ellen, R.; Gellner, E.; Kubca, G. & Mucha, J. et al. (ed.) *Malinowski Between Two Worlds*, pp. 12-148.

KUBICA, G., (1988) 'Malinowski Year's in Poland', en Ellen, R.; Gellner, E.; Kubica, G. & Mucha, J. (ed.) *Malinowski between two worlds,* pp. 89-104.

KUPER, A., (1973) *Antropología y Antropólogos. La Escuela Británica, 1922-1972*. Barcelona, Anagrama.

KUPER, A., (1999) *Among the Anthropologist. History and Context in Anthropology*. London, Athlone Press.

LABOURET, H. (1953) 'L'Echangeet le Commerce dans les Archipels du Pacifique et en Afrique Tropicale' Libro I, Tomo III, *L'Histoire du Commerce* (ed. J. Lacour-Gavet) pp. 9-125, Paris.

LEACH, E. R., (1974) 'La base epistemológica del empirismo de Malinowski', en Firth, R.; Leach E. R., y otros, *Hombre y cultura. La obra de Bronislaw Malinowski*. Madrid, Siglo XXI, pp. 291-312.

LENOIR, R., (1924) 'Les Expeditions Maritimes, Institution Sociale en Mélanesie Occidentale'. *L'Anthropologie*, Tomo 34, pp. 387-410. París.

LEVI-STRAUSS, C. (1949) *Las estructuras elementales del parentesco*. Buenos Aires Eudeba, 1984.

LEVI-STRAUSS, C. (1955) *Tristes Trópicos*. Barcelona, Paidós, 1988.

LOUNSBURY, F. (1965) 'Another view of the Trobriand kinship categories', *American Anthropologist*, 67:142-185, y en W. Goodenough (ed.), *Explorations in Cultural Anthropology*. New York.

MAIR, L., (1974) 'Malinowski y el estudio del cambio social', en Firth, R.; Leach E. R., y otros, 1974. *Hombre y cultura. La obra de Bronislaw Malinowski*. Madrid, Siglo XXI, pp. 249-266.

MALINOWSKI, B. (1912) 'The economic aspects of *Intichiuma* Ceremonies' en R. J. Thornoton and P. Skalník (ed.), *The early writing of Broniwslaw Malinowski. Malinowski's writings, 1904-1914*. Cambridge University Press. (1993)

MALINOWSKI, B., (1913) *The Family Among the Australian Aborigines:A Sociological Study*. Introduction by J. A. Barnes. New York, Schocken, 1963.

MALINOWSKI, B. (1915) '*The Natives of Mailu*'. *Malinowski Among the Magi*. London, Routledge. Edition and Introduction by Michael W. Young. 1988.

MALINOWSKI, B., (1916) 'Baloma:The Spirit of the Dead in the Trobriand Island', en B. Malinowski, *Magic, Science an Religion and Other Essays*. New York, Anchor, 1955.

MALINOWSKI, B. (1920) 'Classificatory Particles in the Language of Kiriwina', *Bulletin of the School of Oriental Studies*, I (4):33-78.

MALINOWSKI, B., (1921) 'The primitive economics of the Trobriand Islanders', *The Economic Journal*, 31, 121:1-16.

MALINOWSKI, B., (1922) *Los Argonautas del Pacífico Occidental*. Barcelona, Península. 1985.

MALINOWSKI, B., (1923) 'El problema del significado en las lenguas primitivas', en Ogden, C. K. y Richards, I. A. (ed.) *El significado del significado*. Buenos Aires, Paidós, pp. 312—360. 1964.

MALINOWSKI, B., (1925) 'Myth in Primitive Psychology' en B. Malinowski (1955) *Magic, Science an Religion and Other Essays*. New York, Anchor.

MALINOWSKI, B., (1926) *Crimen y costumbre en la sociedad salvaje*. Barcelona, Ariel, 1963.

MALINOWSKI, B., (1927 a) *Sexo y represión en la sociedad primitiva*. Buenos Aires, Nueva Visión. 1974.

MALINOWSKI, B., (1927 b) *The Father in Primitive Psycology*. London, Kegan Paul.

MALINOWSKI, B., (1929) *La vida sexual de los salvajes del noreste de la Melanesia.* Madrid, Morata, con prefacio de Havelock Ellis, 1971.

MALINOWSKI, B., (1930) 'Kinship', *Man*, vol. XXX, n° 17.

MALINOWSKI, B., (1931) 'La cultura', en J. S. Kahn (ed.) *El concepto de Cultura. Textos fundamentales.* Barcelona, Anagrama, 1973.

MALINOWSKI, B., (1935) *Jardines de coral y su magia. El cultivo de la tierra y los ritos agrícolas en las islas Trobriand.* Barcelona, Labor. 1977.

MALINOWSKI, B. (1937) 'Culture as a determinant of behavior', en E. D. Adrian and others (ed.), *Factors Determining Human Behavior.* Cambridge, Mass, Harvard University Press, pp. 133-168

MALINOWSKI, B., (1944) *Una teoría científica de la cultura.* Barcelona, Sarpe, 1984.

MALINOWKI, B., (1945) *The Dynamics of Culture Change:An Inquiry into Race Relations in Africa.* Ed. By P.M. Kaberry. New Haven, Yale University Press.

MALINOWSKI, B., (1947) *Freedom and Civilization.* New York, Roy Books.

MALINOWSKI, B., (1955) *Magic, Science an Religion and Other Essays.* New York, Anchor.

MALINOWSKI, B. (1962) 'Myth as a dramatic development of dogma', en *Sex, Culture and Myth*. New York, Harcourt, Brace and World.

MALINOWSKI, B., (1963) *Estudios de psicología primitiva*. Buenos Aires, Paidós.

MALINOWSKI, B., (1967) *Diario de campo de Melanesia*. Madrid, Júcar. 1989.

MALINOWSKI, B., (1975) 'Confesiones de ignorancia y fracaso', en J.R. Llobera (ed.) *La antropología como ciencia*. Barcelona, Anagrama, pp. 129-139.

MALINOWSKI, B., (1995) *Sobre el principi de l'economia del pensament*. Traducción y prologo de Joan Bestard. Barcelona, Icaria.

MALINOWSKI, B. & DE LA FUENTE, J., (1957) *The Economics of a Mexican Market System. An essay in Contemporary Ethnographic and Social Change in a Mexican Valley*. Introduction by S. Drucker Brown. London, Routledge, & Kegan Paul, 1982.

MAUSS, M., (1924) 'Ensayo sobre el don', en *Sociología y Antropología*. Madrid, Tecnos. 1971.

MERCIER, P., (1979) 'Conquistas', en *Historia de la Antropología*. Barcelona, Península, cap. 4, pp. 127-171.

MÉTRAUX, R. (1979) 'Malinowski, Bronislaw', *Enciclopedia Internacional de las Ciencias Sociales*. Madrid, Aguilar.

MUCHA, J., (1988) 'Malinowski and the problems of contemporary civilisation', en Ellen, R., Gellner, E., Kubica, G. & Mucha, J. et al. (ed.) *Malinowski Between Two Worlds*, pp. 149-163.

MURDOCK, G. P., (1943) 'Bronislaw Malinowski', *American Anthropologist*, vol. 45, 441-451.

MURDOCK, G. P., (1949) *Social Structure*. New York.

NADEL, S. F. (1974) 'Malinowski, sobre la magia y la religión', en Firth, R.; Leach E. R., y otros, 1974. *Hombre y cultura. La obra de Bronislaw Malinowski*. Madrid, Siglo XXI, pp. 201-225.

PALUCH, A. J. (1988) 'Malinowski' theory of culture', en Ellen, R., Gellner, E., Kubica, G. & Mucha, J. et al. (ed.) *Malinowski Between Two Worlds*, pp.65-88.

PALUCH, A. J., (1988) 'Bronislaw Malinowski and Cracow anthropology', en Ellen, R.; Gellner, E., Kubica, G. & Mucha, J. et al. (ed.) *Malinowski Between Two Worlds*, pp. 1-11.

PANOFF, M., (1974) *Malinowski y la antropología*. Barcelona, Labor.

PARSONS, T. (1974) 'Malinowski y la Teoría de los Sistemas Sociales' en Firth, R., Leach, E., y otros, *Hombre y cultura. La obra de Bronislaw Malinowski*. Madrid, Siglo XXI, pp. 62-84.

PAYNE, H. (1981) 'Malinowski's Style', en *Proceedings of the American Philosophical Society*. Vol. 125, 6:416-440.

PIDDINGTON, R., (1974) 'La teoría de las necesidades de Malinowski', en Firth, R., Leach, E., y otros, *Hombre y cultura. La obra de Bronislaw Malinowski*. Madrid, Siglo XXI, pp. 39-61.

RICHARDS, A. I., (1943) 'Bronislaw Kaspar Malinowski:Born 1884—Died 1942', *Man*, 43, 1-4.

RICHARDS, A. I., (1974) 'El concepto de cultura en la obra de Malinowski', en Firth, R., Leach, E., y otros, *Hombre y cultura. La obra de Bronislaw Malinowski*. Madrid, Siglo XXI, pp. 19-38.

STOCKING, G. W., (1968) 'Empathy and Antipathy in the Heart of Darkness', *Journal of the History of the Behavioral Sciences*, vol. 4:189-194.

STOCKING, G. W., (1983) 'The Ethnographer's Magic:Fieldwork in British Anthropology, from Tylor to Malinowski', *History of Anthropology*, vol. 1, The University of Wisconsin Press, 70-120.

STOCKING, G. W., (1986) 'Anthropology and The Science of the Irrational. Malinowski's Encounters with Freudian Psychoanalysis', *History of Anthropology*, vol. 4, The University of Wisconsin Press, 13-49.

STOCKING, G. W., (1992) *The Ethnographer's Magic and Other Essays in the History of Anthropology*. The University of Wisconsin Press.

SZACKI, J., (1988) 'Malinowski and the development of Polish social science', en Ellen R., Gellenr, E., Kubica, G.

& Mucha, J. et al. (ed.) *Malinowski Between Two Worlds*, pp. 43-51.

SZTOMPKA, P., (1988) 'From Malinowski to Merton:a case-study in the transmission of ideas', en Ellen, R., Gellner, E., Kubica, G. & Mucha, J. et al. (ed.) *Malinowski Between Two Worlds*, pp. 52-64.

TERRADAS SABORIT, I., 1993. "Realismo etnográfico. Una reconsideración del programa de Bronislaw K. Malinowski", en Bestard i Camps, J. (coord.) *Después de Malinowski*. Tenerife, FAAEE, pp. 117-148.

THORNTON, R. J. & SKALNIK, P. (ed.), (1993) *The Early writing of Bronislaw Malinowski. Malinowski's writings, 1904-1914.* Cambridge University Press.

WARNOTTE, D. (1927) *Les Origines Sociologiques de l'Obligation Contractuelle.* Bruselas, Institut Solvay.

WAYNE MALINOWSKA, H., (1984) 'Bronislaw Malinowski:the influence of various women on his life and works', *Journal of the Anthropological Society of Oxford*, vol. 15:189-203.

WAYNE, H., (ED.) (1995) *The story of a Marriage. The letters of Bronislaw Malinowski and Elsie Masson.* 2 Vol. London, Routledge.

WITTGENSTEIN, L., (1953) *Investigaciones filosóficas.* Barcelona, Crítica, 1988.

YOUNG, M. W. (1988) 'Introduction', B. Malinowski, (1915) *Malinowski Among the Magi. 'The Natives of Mailu'.* London, Routledge.

YOUNG, M. W. (ed.) (1979) *The ethnography of Malinowski. The Trobriand Islands 1915-18*. London, Rutledge and Kegan Paul.

YOUNG, M. W. (1998) *Malinowski's Kiriwina. Fieldwork Photography, 1915-1918*. Chicago, The Chicago University Press.

YOUNG, M. W. (2004) *Malinowski. Odyssey of an Anthropologist, 1884-1920*. Yale University Press.